KAHUKU POINT

TURTLE BAY

SUNSET BEACH

'Ehukai Beach Park

KAHUKU

WAIMEA BAY

LA'IE

Polynesian
Cultural Center

LANIAKEA BEACH

Waimea Falls Park

O'AHU'S HIDDEN HISTORY

Tours Into the Past

HAU'ULA

each Park

Sacred Falls
State Park

PUNALU'U

ILUA

HALE'IWA

Kahana Valley
State Park

MT. KA'ALA

WAHIAWA

Schofield
Barracks

MI

PEARL CITY

WAIPAHU

AIEA

NANAKULI

BOR

MAKAKILO

'EWA

Honolulu
International
Airport

Park

Campbell
Industrial
Park

'EWA BEACH

Barbers Point
Naval Air Station

One'ula
Beach Park

Sand Island
Honolulu Harbor
Downtown Honolulu

RBERS POINT

OTHER BOOKS BY WILLIAM H. DORRANCE

Viscous Hypersonic Flow

Fort Kamehameha: The Story of the Harbor Defenses
of Pearl Harbor

O'AHU'S HIDDEN HISTORY

Tours Into the Past

WILLIAM H. DORRANCE

MUTUAL PUBLISHING

Copyright © 1998
by Mutual Publishing

Library of Congress Catalog Card
Number: 98-66830

First Printing, September 1998
Second Printing, October 1999
2 3 4 5 6 7 8 9

ISBN 1-56647-211-3

Design by Jane Hopkins

Mutual Publishing
1215 Center Street, Suite 210
Honolulu, Hawaii 96816
Telephone (808) 732-1709
Fax (808) 734-4094
e-mail: mutual@lava.net
www.mutualpublishing.com

Printed in Taiwan

O'AHU'S HIDDEN HISTORY
Tours Into the Past

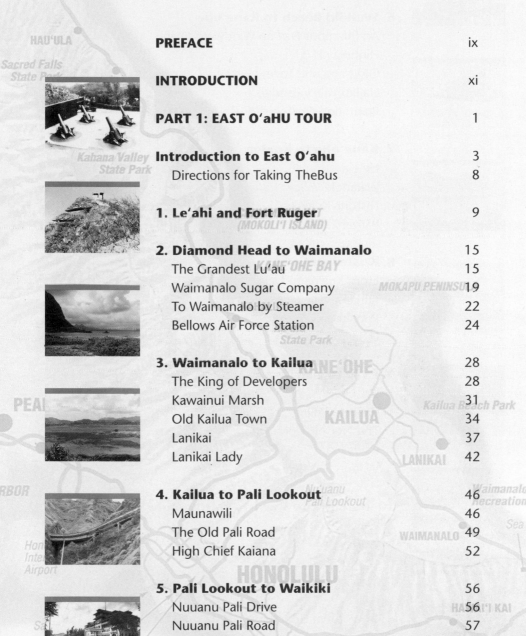

PREFACE

WHEN RESIDENTS OF Oʻahu entertain family and friends as house guests, their visitors are usually given a quick resume of the island's attractions and sometimes a too-quick tour of the island. Guests are then urged to explore the island on their own, armed with a map, a few directions and a guide book.

Our visitors frequently returned with complaints about the guide books. "Why is that place important and located there? How old is that community? Who established the community? And what was that old structure I saw there? What are those places called 'forts' all about?"

I saw a need for a different kind of guide book. This book not only tells you how to find the many interesting places on Oʻahu but why they are located where they are, who first settled there, and what the artifacts found there were intended to be. It can also be read and enjoyed by armchair explorers.

I had a headstart after several years of writing feature stories about Oʻahu locales and personalities for a monthly newspaper. The book contains abridgements of several stories that have appeared since 1991 in *Windward Oahu News*. Each story is timeless and focuses on the history of a locality, artifact, or prominent resident. Together with similar pieces written exclusively for the book, they represent a history of Oʻahu's interesting people, places, and things. My research was supplemented by personally visiting, photographing, and exploring each place.

I wish to thank Leatrice Arakaki (dec.), Sam Caldwell, Tom Fairfull, Pat Garties, Betty Lou Kam, Jack Russell, Peter Smith, and Maile Yardley for answering my many questions that related to their knowledge of O'ahu's past and present. Mrs. Arakaki, Historian, 15th Air Base Wing; Mr. Fairfull, Director, U.S. Army Museum of Hawai'i; and Ms. Kam, Bishop Museum; were instrumental in my obtaining photographs for use in this book; and Mr. Smith shared information he had obtained during his explorations of O'ahu's rugged coastline and interior. My wife, Jan, was a source of constant encouragement and accompanied me on many explorations of the island.

This book could not have been written without the interviews and conversations I held with *kama'aina* (born in Hawai'i) or long-time residents of Hawai'i. I wish to thank Peggy Hickok Hodge, Agnes and John Miholick, Francis S. Morgan, Marsue McShane, and Dr. Frederick Reppun (dec.) for sharing their stories with me.

I am a historian and writer and author of the book, *Fort Kamehameha The Story of the Harbor Defenses of Pearl Harbor.* Several of my articles have appeared in *Historic Hawai'i* magazine and *The Hawaiian Journal of History* in addition to those featured in *Windward Oahu News.*

William H. Dorrance
Kailua, O'ahu, Hawai'i

INTRODUCTION

THE ISLAND OF Oʻahu is a special place. While the balmy weather and beauty of the mountains, flora, beaches, and ocean views are eternal, the contributions of man, past and present, play an important role in the island's mystique.

Oʻahu's culture and history were formed during three overlapping eras. The first, begun some 1300 to 1500 years ago, was that of the Native Hawaiians. It was they who gave the place names that survive to the present. About the fifteenth century, the ruling chief divided Oʻahu into six *moku* (districts) and numerous *ahupuaʻa* (subdivisions of *moku*). Today's judicial districts correspond to the *moku* and the names of the *ahupuaʻa* live on as the names of localities, communities, camps, villages, and towns. Hawaiʻi enjoys the distinction of having the largest percentage of ancient land boundaries and place names of any of the United States.

The locations of today's settlements within the *ahupuaʻa* were largely determined during the era of post-discovery (after 1778) commercial activity. The location of Honolulu is explained by the fact that in the century following 1778 it possessed the only sheltered harbor in the islands. The location of settlements in the rest of the island were mostly determined by nineteenth-century plantations. Workers were housed in nearby villages (called "camps"). The sugarcane plantations are gone but numerous former camps survive as today's villages, towns, and places.

The last determining era began in 1898 with the annexation by the United States. The U.S. military arrived soon after and currently occupies about one-quarter of Oʻahu's land. The establishment of the numerous barracks, bases, forts, and stations was a twentieth century, post-annexation, activity. Even so, much of this is now history.

Forts Armstrong, Ruger, Weaver, Kamehameha, and Barrette have been abandoned by the military, most to the city or state, and much of their concrete remains became monuments to the past after the Army's Coast Artillery branch was disbanded in 1950.

The exploration of O'ahu is divided into three parts: East O'ahu, Central O'ahu, and West O'ahu.

An excellent municipal bus system, called "TheBus", serves almost every place described during each of the three tours. The bus routes (referred to as "bus numbers") and travel times are given in the introduction to each of the tours. However, routes and schedules can change, and those contemplating the tours using this method are urged to verify the routes with TheBus Information Center (848-5555).

PART ONE

EAST OʻAHU TOUR

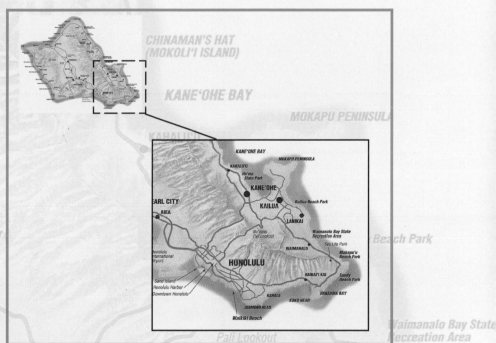

Driving time: Three hours minimum plus time for stops for lunch, beach and side trips.

TheBus time: Four hours plus time for stops for beach and visits to attractions.

INTRODUCTION TO EAST O'AHU

WHILE YOU CAN join the tour at any point along the way, for simplicity's sake we will assume your tour begins in Waikiki. Your first destination is the trail head for the climb to Diamond Head Lookout located on the ocean side crest of Diamond Head Crater. Starting in Waikiki, drive east along Kalakaua to the intersection with Monsarrat Avenue (the Honolulu Zoo corner). Turn left onto Monsarrat and proceed 1-1/4 miles until it becomes Diamond Head Road. Follow Diamond Head Road around the mauka (inland) side of the crater about 1/4 mile to the access road to the crater that is clearly marked with a sign. Turn right onto the access road, follow it through a tunnel into the interior of the crater, and proceed about 1/4 mile to the designated parking area. A paved pathway leads from the parking area to the foot of the Diamond Head Trail that rises to the viewing site on the crest.

After visiting the lookout, retrace your path from the interior of the crater to Diamond Head Road and turn right toward the ocean. After about 1/4 mile turn left on Kahala Avenue. For the next 1-1/2 miles you will be passing through Kahala, one of the most affluent communities on O'ahu. Turn left when you arrive at Kealaolu Avenue. After 3/4 miles along Kealaolu Avenue, bordered on the right by Waialae Country Club where the Hawaiian Open Golf Tournament is held each year, you arrive at the access road to enter Kalanianaole Highway, Highway 72. Turn right onto the access road and enter the highway going east.

The melodious "Kalanianaole" refers to Prince Jonah Kuhio Kalaniana'ole (1871-1922). Kuhio Avenue and Kuhio Beach in Waikiki and the Federal Building in Honolulu are named for him.

The next 5-1/2 miles take you through the residential suburbs of Honolulu known as Aina Haina and Hawai'i Kai, the latter a development begun in the late 1950s by ambitious tycoon Henry J. Kaiser (1882-1967). After passing Hawai'i Kai you arrive at Koko Head Crater on the right. Hanauma Bay State Underwater Park, formed by a long extinct volcanic crater, comes next. To wade on the sandy bottom here is to experience the rare treat of having colorful and exotic fish swim about your legs. Snorkling and scuba diving in deeper waters reveal a diverse array of ocean fish that can be seen nowhere else in Hawai'i.

Be warned that fees are collected for parking and for visiting the beach park should you choose to stop. As of March 1998, the parking fee was $1.00, admission was $3.00 for visitors, and two-way trolley ticket to the beach was $1.50 for adults and $1.00 for children. Expect fees to change from time to time, however. The revenues are used to offset the cost of maintaining the park. The park is closed for maintenance on Wednesday morning until noon.

Next you will pass Sandy Beach, rated third for sunning and viewing by O'ahu residents but not very safe for body and board surfing by neophytes. After Sandy Beach you must resist taking your eyes off the road to view some of the most rugged coastline on O'ahu. The sights of the ocean waves crashing ashore are outstanding.

Three miles after passing Sandy Beach you are rounding the turn at Makapu'u Point. The highway is elevated and as you make the turn to descend into Waimanalo you see Kaohikaipu and Manana Islands offshore, the three peaks on Mount Olomana in the left distance, and Mokapu Peninsula in the far right-center distance. Sea Life Park is on the immediate left as you prepare to move on into Waimanalo *ahupua'a*.

Sea Life Park includes an aquatic display of ocean animals and birds. The animals perform at the urging of their trainers and the visitor cannot fail to be impressed at their intelligence. This commercial attraction has long been an employer of many residents of Waimanalo.

Continuing your tour, Waimanalo Beach Park, rated fourth for family fun by O'ahu residents, is next followed by the outskirts of the Waimanalo settlement and Waimanalo Bay State Recreation Area. The settlement on the left consist of the Hawaiian home lands set aside by the government for Native Hawaiians in response to 1919 legislation introduced in Congress by Prince Kuhio. Finally, 4-3/4 miles after rounding Makapu'u Point, you arrive at a substantial polo field on the left and the entrance to Bellows Air Force Station on the right.

Returning from a drive into the Bellows reservation if a weekend or holiday, turn right onto Kalanianaole Highway. After 3/4 mile you are passing through Waimanalo settlement, the closest rural community to Honolulu. The residents intend to keep it that way as chickens, cattle, and horses populate the many back-country farms and ranches. Cash crops are grown on small truck farms scattered throughout the *ahupua'a.*

After driving 3-1/2 miles east on Kalanianaole Highway, you reach the intersection with Kailua Road. Castle Hospital is diagonally across the way at the intersection. Turn right onto Kailua Road and drive about a mile to the entrance to Kailua town. On the way to Kailua you will pass a row of churches on the left. Nestled among the churches and next to the YMCA is Ulupo Heiau, a State Historic Site. The churches surround the *heiau* to complete a row of temples the religions of which date back to before the time of Kamehameha I (1758?-1819). Those who visit the *heiau* can park in the YMCA parking lot. A short walk leads to the substantial *heiau.*

You will know you have reached the entrance to Kailua town when you cross over a modest concrete bridge (dates to 1940) to encounter the stoplight at at Hamakua Road. Continue on Kailua Road which veers to the right at the next intersection.

You proceed through downtown Kailua about 3/4 mile until you reach a stoplight where Kailua Road turns left toward the ocean. You will know that you are on the right road by the long row of mature ironwood trees that hug the road on the left. (It is a minor fact of history that these trees were planted by ranch hands back in 1921 to serve as a windbreak for the pasture that was then on the right.) Turn left at the stoplight and continue less than a 1/2 mile until you reach the intersection with S. Kalaheo Road. Directly across the street is Kalapawai Store (established in 1932). To the left of the store is the first of three access roads into parking areas for Kailua Beach.

Turn right at Kalapawai Store onto S. Kalaheo to continue the tour. Very shortly you will turn left, then right onto Kawailoa Road and pass over a narrow concrete bridge. Another parking area for Kailua Beach is to the left just after you pass Buzz's Steakhouse on the right. Continue a short distance with the forested greens on the left until you reach an intersection where you turn left toward the ocean onto Alala Road. Very shortly you encounter another beach parking area. A busy boat-launching ramp is located at this end of Kailua Beach. Many fishermen, commercial and otherwise, launch their trailer-hauled boats here.

A short stretch of winding and rising Alala road takes you around the bend into the cul-de-sac roads serving the community known as Lanikai. As you round the point on Alala road to enter Lanikai you encounter a fork in the road. From this point on the road is one-way. The right hand road, Aalapapa, runs 1-1/4 mile into the settlement until it reaches the end. The road then becomes Mokulua and returns to the entrance to Lanikai.

Here's how to find and visit Lanikai Beach. Public beach access paths are located opposite almost every cross road between Aalapapa and Mokulua Roads. The best beach locations are about midway along Mokulua between Onekea Drive at the Bellows end and Mokumanu Drive at the Kailua end. Park your car on the right or left and off the road and bikeway. Access to the beach is free for all comers.

Retrace your drive into Lanikai until you reach the intersection at Kalapawai Store. Instead of turning left onto Kailua Road continue straight ahead on S. Kalaheo for about 3/4 mile until you reach an intersection with a stoplight. A sign indicates that you turn left here to go to the Pali. Turn left and pass through three stoplights and most of Kailua town.

Drive toward Honolulu on Kailua Road until reaching the intersection with Kalanianaole Highway at Castle Hospital. Kailua Road now becomes Kalanianaole Highway for a short run. About 3/4 mile after this intersection there is a stoplight at Maunawili Road. Those wishing to experience the beauties of an earlier time should turn left here and enter Maunawili Valley, always bearing left at each intersection encountered. It is possible to drive about three miles into the interior.

Return to the intersection with Kalanianaole Highway and turn left toward the Pali. At the second stoplight the highway to Honolulu becomes the Pali Road. The winding ascent to the Pali tunnels and lookout begins here.

The access road to the Pali Lookout is located on the right about 1-1/4 mile after exiting the tunnels. Keep to the right in order to be prepared for the sharp right turn. The access road is an improved portion of the old Nuuanu Pali Road that led to the pass and Pali Lookout. Follow this road to the parking area at the lookout. Be warned that the lookout is always quite windy and many a hat has irretrievably been lost here.

After returning to the Honolulu-bound lane of the Pali Highway pull into the left lane. About 1/2 mile after you enter the highway, turn left to enter Nuuanu Pali Drive. The drive winds through a bower of trees for almost three miles before rejoining the Nuuanu Pali Road.

After rejoining the Pali Highway (Nuuanu Pali Road on some maps) you will enter a residential area starting at Wood Street. Once under the Wyllie Street overpass, you continue Honolulu bound until the Pali Road jogs left and becomes Bishop Street. Pass through one of the cleanest and most pleasant downtown areas of any major city until you reach S. Nimitz Highway. Turn left onto S. Nimitz toward Waikiki Beach. Soon S. Nimitz becomes Ala Moana Boulevard. About 1-3/4 mile after this, you are passing the Ala Moana Shopping Center on the left and Ala Moana Beach Park on the right.

Take the right fork before crossing the Ala Wai Canal to enter Waikiki Beach. Turn right onto Kalia Road at the stoplight. A 1/4 mile drive takes you through the well-manicured expanse of Fort DeRussy. The two towers of the all-military Hale Koa Hotel are midway along Kalia Road on the right followed by scenes of the lightly forested approach to the beach. Just before you reach the intersection with Saratoga Road you see Battery Randolph that houses the U.S. Army Museum of Hawaii. Entrance to a convenient parking lot is on the left opposite the museum.

After passing, or stopping to visit the museum, resume the tour by turning left onto Saratoga Road from Kalia Road to return to Kalakaua Avenue. Turn right onto Kalakaua and soon you will be back at your starting point. The total mileage, including side trips, adds up to about seventy miles.

DIRECTIONS FOR TAKING THEBUS

The route does not vary. All it takes to make the tour using TheBus is to chose the right combination of buses to board along the way.

Assume that you start again in Waikiki Beach. Board bus no. 22 on Kuhio Avenue (no buses run on Kalakaua Avenue). Those who choose to make the Diamond Head Lookout climb should exit bus no. 22 at the well-marked access road to the right off Diamond Head Road. A one-mile walk will take them to the trail head. Because the buses do not enter the access road it will be necessary to retrace your steps to reboard bus no. 22 at Diamond Head Road to continue the tour.

Bus no. 22 terminates at Sea Life Park. Transfer there to Kailua-bound bus no. 57. In Kailua transfer to bus no. 70 bound for Kailua Beach Park and Lanikai. After enjoying the Lanikai loop, exit bus no. 70 back in Kailua diagonally across the road from where you boarded it, and transfer to Honolulu-bound bus no. 57 that returns to Ala Moana via the Nuuanu Pali Road. At Ala Moana transfer to any one of buses no. 8, 19, 20, 47, or 68 to return to your starting point.

TheBus does not make the side trips into Bellows AFS, to the Pali Lookout, or along Nuuanu Pali Drive.

Be sure to ask for a transfer when you board the first bus. Carry a supply of dollar bills for fares if you plan to make one or more stops along the way. Each stop requires a fare payment when you reboard the bus and the drivers do not make change. Buses are scheduled to arrive at stops at about thirty-minute or one-hour intervals depending on the routes and time of day. Allow at least three hours for a stop to visit the Diamond Head Lookout and at least one hour for each beach stop. Call (808) 848-5555 for up-to-date schedule information.

CHAPTER ONE

LE'AHI AND FORT RUGER

YOUR FIRST DESTINATION is the Diamond Head Lookout located on the ocean side crest of Diamond Head Crater. The lookout is one of the most accessible and popular viewing sites on O'ahu. The modest climb can be made by young and old who are in reasonably good physical condition and is made by hundreds every day. The trailhead is located inside the crater below the lookout. Plan on taking one and one-half hours to make the climb and descent, plus the time you take to enjoy the views of metropolitan Honolulu and surroundings. Take a flashlight with you. The rising trail follows a switchback path to two stairways linked by a 225-foot tunnel. The trail ends with a spiral stairway in the dark interior of a four-level, buried, concrete observation station. The dark stairway leads to the crest. At the end of the climb, the view of Honolulu from the 760-foot summit is unsurpassed. Caution: if the 76-step and 99-step stairways are daunting, don't attempt the climb.

Why and when was the substantial underground concrete complex constructed? Most visitors to the site correctly speculate that it had a military purpose but few are correct about guessing its age. The most frequent guess is that it was some kind of World War II gun emplacement. Not so, as the following story explains.

You know it as "Diamond Head" but the long-ago Native Hawaiians knew it as "Le'ahi," perhaps a contraction of the word "Laeahi" meaning brow *(lae)* of the tuna *(ahi)*. When you contemplate the crater's silhouette from Waikiki Beach, you can see the resemblance. Most people nowadays refer to the location as "Diamond Head," a name given to it by naive British sailors in the nineteenth century. There were and are no diamonds within the crater.

When the United States annexed Hawai'i in 1898 it added harbor defenses to its responsibilities. Honolulu and Pearl Harbors had to be protected from hostile bombardment or, in the extreme, from invasion. One of the Honolulu Harbor defense forts occupied Diamond Head Crater and was named Fort Ruger. Among the weapons located at Fort Ruger was an eight-cannon battery of 12-inch caliber mortars emplaced on the inland flanks of Diamond Head and named Battery Harlow. The mortars could hurl 700-pound deck piercing projectiles to a range of eleven miles. The crater's wall would conceal their presence from an offshore enemy vessel and protect the cannon and cannoneers from any retaliatory and flat naval fire of that day.

Pit A of Battery Harlow showing four of the eight 12-inch mortars emplaced at the battery. Pit B, to the left and not shown, contained the four other mortars. The battery structure still exists and is used for storage by the Hawaii Army National Guard. The mortars were removed by 1950. (*U.S. Army Museum of Hawai'i*)

However, the crater's walls also prevented gun pointers located at the battery from seeing the offshore targets, so some sort of forward-based observation station was required. Before radar was invented the target location was determined using powerful telescopes. Battery Harlow, completed in 1910, required such target sighting in order to point the mortars, and the battery's optical observation station was located at Le'ahi. Plotting of target positions was done at the observation station and the target coordinates, determined by triangulation and using a scale map, were telephoned back to Battery Harlow and were used to point the large cannons.

The task of constructing a suitable observation station at Le'ahi was begun in 1908. There was no modern earth-moving equipment available in those times and much of the work was done with pick and shovel.

Easier access to the crater floor was created by tunnelling through the crater wall. A 580-foot tunnel was dug not far from Battery Harlow's location. Narrow-gauge tramway tracks were put down for transporting construction material across the crater floor to a location below the site of the station. Army mules pulled the tramway cars.

A narrow switchback pathway was carved up the inner slope of the crater to an elevation of 560 feet. The observation post was to be at 760 feet, so a winch platform was built at this level such that construction material could be lifted and lowered by cable.

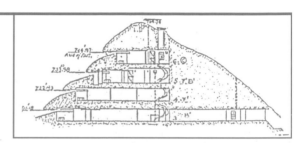

War Department drawing of the observation station constructed at Le'ahi. The station was completed and turned over to the Coast Artillery in March 1911. *(National Archives)*

The remaining 200 feet to the summit was traversed by, successively, a 76-step concrete stairway, a 225-foot sloping tunnel and a 99-step concrete stairway. At this level a massive excavation was undertaken to create a four-level underground complex. Thousands of cubic yards of lava, earth, and stone were excavated. The observation station was completed and turned over to coast artillery troops in March 1911, long before World War I.

The lowest level of the four-level complex was assigned to a two-gun battery of 14-inch guns located at Fort DeRussy on Waikiki Beach and named Battery Randolph. Target locations for Battery Randolph's guns were plotted here. The next level belonged to the Fort DeRussy commander. It was he who determined which of Fort DeRussy's guns should fire at which targets.

The third level was assigned to Battery Harlow's artillerymen. Both target sighting and coordinate plotting was done here. The top level belonged to the overall battle commander. He coordinated the efforts of all the batteries assigned to defend Honolulu harbor. All four levels are connected by a winding spiral staircase.

Evidence of the complex is not easily seen from the ground or ocean. This was deliberate. For an enemy to locate and knock out this station would be to blind Battery Harlow's 12-inch seacoast mortars.

Major Eben Eveleth Winslow (1866-1928), the engineering officer under whom the Le'ahi observation station and Battery Harlow were completed, was a key man in the Army Corps of Engineers' plans. In 1911 the Corps of Engineers transferred him from Hawai'i to the Panama Canal Zone where he supervised the construction of the coast defense fortifications that were to protect the Atlantic and Pacific entrances to the canal.

Brigadier General Winslow retired with honors in 1920 to his family homestead in Tennessee where he died in 1928. His wife, Anne Goodwin Winslow, survived him by many years and, while living on the homestead, established an international reputation of her own as an essayist, author, poet, and literary critic.

Fort Ruger was one of three forts constructed before World War I to protect Honolulu Harbor. The other forts were Fort DeRussy at Waikiki Beach and Fort Armstrong at the entrance to the harbor. They formed a powerful triumvirate. Fort Ruger's mortars threatened armored decks with near-vertical plunging fire, Fort DeRussy's high powered guns threatened the armored sides of enemy vessels, and Fort Armstrong's controlled submarine mines were a last ditch defense

Le'ahi Observation Station. The station was concealed from view as much as possible in order to make it difficult to precisely fix its position. The uppermost structure supported a World War II radar. *(U.S. Army Museum of Hawai'i)*

as they threatened the hulls and bottoms of vessels attempting to force an entry into the harbor. This scheme of harbor defenses had been perfected by the Army during the last decades of the nineteenth century and over seventy such forts were established to protect the nation's harbors. It was natural that the Army should seek to protect O'ahu's harbors following the annexation of the Republic of Hawaii in 1898.

However, Hawai'i owes much to then Secretary of War William H. Taft (1857-1930) for the establishment of these defenses on O'ahu. Following the annexation several boards of officers had recommended harbor defenses for Honolulu and Pearl Harbors but there was little agreement among them as to specifics. Something more was needed at a high level to resolve differences, so in 1905 President Theodore Roosevelt (1858-1919) convened a board of inquiry to settle the questions. The board's chairman, Secretary Taft (later President Taft in 1909-1913), visited O'ahu to see for himself what the required defenses might be. He also visited the Philippines and Panama to inspect at first hand the need for harbor defenses in those localities. Out of his trip came a thorough report of the defenses required that included an upgrading of weaponry at mainland harbor defense forts.

Taft's 1906 report resulted in Congress appropriating funds for the defenses of Honolulu and Pearl Harbor. Forts Ruger, DeRussy, Armstrong, and Kamehameha were the result.

Fort Kamehameha, now incorporated into the Hickam Air Force Base reservation, was situated on near-barren land next to the entrance

Secretary of War William Howard Taft on his inspection trip to Oahu in 1905. The lady on the right is Alice Roosevelt, daughter of President Theodore Roosevelt, who accompanied Taft and his party. Taft went on to visit the Philippines and returned via the Isthmus of Panama. The Army fortified each of these localities following his inspection trip. The island of Corregidor in Manila Bay is one of the post-Taft fortifications. *(Hawai'i State Archives)*

to Pearl Harbor. Remote from the urban area at the time, the reservation was large enough to accommodate a mortar battery, long-range guns, and submarine mine facilities all at one fort. The Pearl Harbor defense concept resembled in every way the concept employed to protect Honolulu Harbor.

CHAPTER TWO

DIAMOND HEAD TO WAIMANALO

YOU ARE HEADED for the *ahupua'a* of Waimanalo after leaving Diamond Head Crater. The picturesque drive along Kalanianaole Highway, route 72, skirts the coastline much of the way. Soon you are rounding Makapu'u Point before descending into Waimanalo.

View of Waimanalo *ahupua'a* from lookout opposite Sea Life Park. The three peaks of Mount Olomana and a part of Mokapu Peninsula are visible in the distance. Also visible is the University of Hawaii Makai Research Station pier. *(W. H. Dorrance)*

You can capture a broad view of Waimanalo *ahupua'a* from the lookout on the ocean side of the highway opposite Sea Life Park. Pause here to enjoy the view and to contemplate a story of a grand visit to Waimanalo that took place over one hundred years ago.

THE GRANDEST LU'AU

High Chief John Adams Cummins (1835-1913) was filled with apprehensions when, in October 1875, he was summoned by dowager Queen Emma (1836-1885), widow of King Kamehameha IV (1834-1863). Cummins had supported his Royal School classmate and winning candidate David Kalakaua (1836-1891) in the 1874 elections for the crown against losing candidate, Queen Emma, and Cummins had no reason to believe that Emma's wounds had healed. Nevertheless, Cummins obeyed the royal summons and was delighted with his reception. All was forgiven by the queen.

Cummins had been a close friend of the late King Kamehameha IV and had often entertained the king and his queen, Emma, at his home in Waimanalo so it was natural that she should turn to him with her latest request. Queen Emma asked Cummins to arrange and accompany her on a royal tour of O'ahu and he was pleased to oblige. The tour was to lead to the grandest *lu'au* (Hawaiian feast) that he could arrange, and he was an expert. Cummins was lord or *konohiki* (headman) of the crown lands of the ancient *ahupua'a* of Waimanalo and he had considerable resources at his disposal, including his fine herd of riding horses. Waimanalo was to be the first stop on the queen's round-the-island tour and Cummins was determined to make the visit a history-making one.

High Chief John Adams Cummins. Cummins shrewdly invested his inheritance and profits from his plantation in real estate. He built and owned the office building block once located at the corner of Fort and Merchant streets in downtown Honolulu. *(Hawaii State Archives)*

Queen Emma's entourage measured up to the scale of Cummins' plans. Her mounted procession consisted of over two hundred Hawaiians including one hundred and forty Hawaiian ladies riding astride and dressed in colorful *pa'u* riding habits (skirt worn by female horseback riders). Several chiefs joined the procession and the queen was accompanied by a steward managing twenty special retainers who discreetly guarded the queen around the clock. She, her mother, chiefs, and, of course, High Chief Cummins led the parade. All were mounted and garbed in colorful clothing and *lei*. The procession made a magnificent sight as it left the queen's residence in Honolulu.

Cummins had chosen November 5, 1875, Guy Fawkes Day, as the starting date, a concession to Queen Emma's known preference for English customs. The procession got started early after a sumptuous breakfast at the queen's residence. Cummins' home in Waimanalo was to be the first stop on the itinerary.

By late afternoon the procession had saluted the *hula* god Malei at Makapu'u Head (since replaced by the lighthouse) and begun their descent into Waimanalo. Cummins had prepared a grand greeting. Six mounted knights in red costumes and visors met the parade and presented arms. Every 300 yards the procession passed under an arch with overhead burning letters that spelled out a Hawaiian slogan. The knights, carrying torches, led the queen and followers through the arches and on to Cummins' home where their arrival was greeted by trumpeters.

Two spacious *lanai* had been constructed, with an overhead cover of palm fronds, each suitable to accommodate 200 guests. A *lu'au* began at 5:30 p.m. Four chefs presided and tables were prepared heavily-laden with fish, fowl, meats, coffee, tea, chocolates, desserts and other specialties that delighted the eye and stomach. It took three hours to do justice to the lavish presentation. At 8:30 p.m. the entertainment began. Fireworks, rockets, and bonfires in the heights of the *pali* (cliff or side of a mountain) provided a dramatic background for the all-night festivities. Three teams of *hula* dancers and singers alternated throughout the night and the food tables were kept replenished. Breakfast was served at 8:00 a.m. and, incredibly, was well-attended.

The festivities had barely begun. Cummins was a skilled entertainment director. One half of the entourage was dispatched into the backwoods to gather *maile* and fruits for fashioning *lei*. The other half retired to the beach where an exhibition of net-casting had been prepared for the queen's amusement. *Honu* (turtle), *'ula* (spiny lobster), *uhu* (parrotfish), *palani* (surgeonfish), *he'e* (squid), *manini* (striped surgeonfish), *humuhumu* (triggerfish), and other denizens of the sea were harvested by the expert fishermen, both men and women.

These activities were followed by a special swimming exhibition. Puha Stream had long been dammed, creating a large pond. Cummins arranged to have the dam breached at a suitable time and four expert swimmers struggled successfully to swim across the swift torrent. Each was rewarded by the queen with a handsome prize. Following this exhibition she and her entourage went for a decorous swim. Then it was time for the evening *lu'au*.

The tables were heavy with cuts from ten hogs, one bullock, turkeys and ducks too numerous to count, and fish of all descriptions. All-night entertainment began at 8:30 p.m. as before, and the surroundings were lit by blue-colored torches. Champion *hula* dancers from around the island participated.

Next morning's breakfast was not so well attended. It seems that many were laid low by an excess consumption of the pork. It didn't matter for long. Soon all were up to participate in the day's amusements arranged by Chief Cummins. First there was horse racing, using several fine horses from his large herd. Wagers were made by many observers. By the end of the racing everybody was awake and ready for come-what-may.

As for the queen, she indulged in some target shooting under Cummins' tutelage. He reported that her marksmanship was such that she could hit a target at a range of 140 yards. After bathing in a mountain stream, the queen freshened up for the evening's *lu'au*. If anything, that evening the food and entertainment surpassed that of the previous two nights. However, in the morning it would be time to move on.

Next morning, after breakfast, the assembly left for Kane'ohe via Wailea Point (between today's Bellows AFS and Lanikai). As they passed the point into what is now called Lanikai, they rode through a burning arch that provided a dramatic exit from Waimanalo.

Local natives attended the *lu'au* and brought more than enough *ho'okupu* (gifts of food). Such was their generosity that Cummins arranged for the excess to be taken by schooner to future stops of the tour or back to the queen's residence in Honolulu.

Of course, Waimanalo wasn't the only reception on the queen's tour, but it was by far the best and most lavish given that Cummins was *konohiki* of Waimanalo. The tour proceeded with stops at Kane'ohe, Waikane, Kahana, Hau'ula, Kapaha, La'ie, Kahuku, Waimea, Waialua, Waipi'o, and Moanalua. Every host had been alerted in advance by Chief Cummins and all were prominent Hawaiians.

As Chief Cummins summed it up: "It is unlikely that such (a tour) will ever be repeated."

For almost one hundred years Waimanalo *ahupua'a* was dominated by a now-gone sugar plantation. The sugarmill stood near where the present day Korean drive-in restaurant is located. This company holds an important place in Native Hawaiian history, as told in the following story.

WAIMANALO SUGAR COMPANY

By any measure expatriate Englishman Thomas Cummins was a bon vivant. Sometime before 1835 he married the high chiefess Kaumakaokane and, through her influence, obtained a royal patent to an estate on crown lands in Waimanalo *ahupua'a* that he named "Mauna Rose." There he raised thoroughbred horses, entertained visiting dignitaries and royalty, and lived the comfortable life of a sportsman and gentleman farmer. To be invited to sit at the Cummins' table was to experience the joys of the rich combination of Hawaiian and English cuisine. It was a good life.

In 1835 a son, John Adams Cummins, was born to the convivial couple. John's mother, Kaumakaokane, was descended from a Big Island line of high chiefs and was a distant cousin of Kamehameha I. It was natural that young John was enrolled in the Royal School with schoolmates William C. Lunalilo (1833-1874) and David Kalakaua, who later became the sixth and seventh monarchs of Hawai'i.

Cummins proved his loyalty to his schoolmate when he supported David Kalakaua's candidacy as he opposed Dowager Queen Emma in the election of 1874. Such was the strength of the friendship that John A. Cummins later served as King Kalakaua's minister of foreign affairs.

Thomas Cummins and his son had entertained every monarch from Kamehameha III (1814-1854) at Mauna Rose. When John A. Cummins took over management of the estate from his father in 1855 he continued the tradition of lavish hospitality. However, the son was much more than a gentleman farmer. The Reciprocity Treaty of 1876 allowed free importation of Hawaiian-produced raw sugar into the United States. In 1877, with the approval of his friend King

Kalakaua, he enlarged his leaseholdings to include almost the entire *ahupua'a* of Waimanalo. By 1880 he had chartered the Waimanalo Sugar Company, planted hundreds of acres of cane, and ordered the machinery for a modern mill. Its operation started on May 10, 1881 and thus began 66 years of plantation life in Waimanalo.

A three-foot narrow gauge plantation railroad was built to haul harvested cane from the fields, supplies from the plantation pier to the mill, and raw sugar to the pier for shipment to Honolulu. This railroad system grew to some ten miles of track before being displaced by motor trucks in late 1944. In 1882 a youth and then a worker were crushed beneath the locomotive and cars in two separate accidents. These fatalities were the first accidental railroad deaths in the Kingdom of Hawai'i. No traces of this picturesque railroad remain.

John A. Cummins was one of the first of the enlightened plantation managers. He saw the need to house his workers and their

Locomotive OLOMANA hauling harvested sugarcane to the Waimanalo mill. This locomotive served from 1885 until 1945 when it was replaced by motor trucks. The locomotive has been restored and is exhibited in a mainland museum. *(Hawaii Sugar Planters' Association)*

dependents humanely and to supply after-work diversions and entertainment. In 1883 he built a large gymnasium-auditorium that housed a library and was the location for band concerts, dancing, and social gatherings for workers and their families. Nothing remains of this building.

In 1885 Cummins relinquished control of the plantation to the plantation's agent, W. G. Irwin & Company, owned by Honolulu businessman William G. Irwin. However, Cummins continued to manage the plantation that cultivated sugarcane on some 5,000 acres of leased lands. By 1894 Cummins was replaced by George Chalmers who, in turn, was replaced with his son George Chalmers, Jr. within a few years.

In 1915, during the senior Chalmers' management, coastal steamer shipments were replaced by motor trucks. The molasses was hauled by tanker truck to the Honolulu docks and the raw sugar was hauled to the Honolulu Sugar Company's refinery in 'Aiea.

A new sugarmill was constructed in 1922 and the supply of irrigation waters was greatly increased. In 1924-25 a team of hardy Koreans dug a two-mile long tunnel at an elevation of 180 feet through the Honolulu-side flank of Mount Olomana. Heavy duty pumps lifted water to the mouth of the tunnel from the junction of Maunawili Stream and Kawainui Marsh. The fresh water flowed downhill through the tunnel to a reservoir in Waimanalo. A pump house survives near the mouth of the tunnel, leaving a ghostly impression in the mountainside jungle. When the plantation shut down, the pump house was abandoned with electric pumps intact.

It was during the Irwin Company's ownership that the Victorian-style house, sometimes called the "Hedemann House" (for later occupants), was built by Irwin deep in the inner regions of Maunawili Valley. Since Irwin sold out to C. Brewer & Company in 1910, this house dates from sometime before then.

In the years 1923-1927 Dr. Carl F. Reppun (father of the late Dr. Fred Reppun) was Territorial physician serving the Ko'olaupoko

House constructed sometime before 1911 in Maunawili Valley by William G. Irwin, owner of Waimanalo Sugar Company. House is still used as a private residence. The unpaved and long-neglected government road into Waimanalo starts in front of this house. *(W. H. Dorrance)*

Judicial District that ran from south of Waimanalo north to Kualoa. Waimanalo plantation had a clinic but no physician, and relied on Doctor Reppun for medical care. He would drive his car from his residence near Wailau Point to the Hedemann House where he would be met with a plantation horse. Then, on horseback, he would travel the rutted government road from the house down into Waimanalo.

Manager George Chalmers, Jr. died in 1935 and was replaced with Mr. George Y. Bennett. When Bennett resigned in 1943 the plantation was nearing its end. Waimanalo Sugar Company was a small plantation by Hawai'i's standards and never produced more than 13,000 tons of sugar in any year. After struggling for years to keep the plantation profitable, C. Brewer & Company closed it down in 1947 and an exotic era passed for rural Waimanalo.

The sugar company is gone but memories related to it live on. The colorful little steamers that connected the plantation to Honolulu were also a piece of the history of bygone days.

To Waimanalo by Steamer

Before 1900 Windward O'ahu was isolated from the docks and commercial warehouses in Honolulu. The Pali road had been marginally improved, but the steep passage was a dangerous challenge for the horse-and-buggy transportation of that day, and a bottleneck to progress. Coastal schooners and steamers (called "coasters" in the vernacular of the time) were the solution to this problem.

Plantation owner and manager John A. Cummins constructed a pier at the shore of what is now Waimanalo Beach Park. (This pier was located opposite the intersection of Huli Street and Kalanianaole Highway. Nothing remains of it.) The plantation railroad connected the pier with the mill location. Soon the coastal steamer *Waimanalo,* 49 tons displacement, was making regular weekly calls at the pier.

King Kalakaua lost no time visiting his friend's plantation. In 1882 the *Waimanalo* deposited Kalakaua at the pier where he boarded a prettily-decorated plantation railroad train that transported him to the waiting crowd at Cummins' home, Mauna Rose. It was the king's first ride on the railroad and he was to return several times to repeat the experience.

King Kalakaua was known to seek out visits to plantations throughout the islands that could provide railroad transportation. He regarded their building and use as an indication of the advancements enjoyed by his small kingdom, and was proud of its railroads.

By 1900 John Cummins had replaced the old *Waimanalo* with a larger coastal steamer owned by the plantation and named for himself. The *J. A. Cummins* displaced some 79 tons and called the Waimanalo pier her home port. Windward Oʻahu residents were accustomed to her coming and going as she picked up cargo at Heeia plantation's pier in Kaneʻohe Bay, as well as making regular stops at the Waimanalo landing. The *J. A. Cummins* served until 1915 when the motor truck and improved roads replaced it.

At the turn of the century the islands were served by twenty registered coastal schooners and five registered coastal steamers, including the *J. A. Cummins*. All of these vessels displaced less than 100 tons (many far less), and because of their small size an inter-island voyage made with them could be a perilous adventure. Most were captained and crewed by native Hawaiians.

Seventeen larger (200 to 600 tons displacement) inter-island steamers plied the ocean between island ports. Many of these vessels made stops at the Waimanalo pier. They were the chief means of transporting bulk goods and the largest among them served until World War II. After the war, barges and airplanes replaced the steamers, and by 1952 trucks replaced all of the railroads.

The 53-ton coaster *Upolu* that served the Kohala coast plantations. Note the sails that were deployed to save fuel whenever winds were favorable. The *J. A. Cummins* was similar to this vessel. *(R. Renton Hind)*

The most dramatic visit to Waimanalo landing occurred in August 1906. The luxury liner *Manchuria* missed her landfall at Makapu'u Point and ran aground not far off Waimanalo landing. When sunrise revealed the liner's plight, the plantation rallied to the rescue. The ship's boats were met at Waimanalo landing by trains made up of plantation locomotives and flat cars, and the shipwrecked passengers were hauled to the warm hospitality awaiting them at the manager's residence. It wasn't Honolulu, but no doubt the anxious passengers remembered their introduction to Hawaiian *aloha* for the rest of their lives. The plantation workers dropped everything to make their impromptu visit a memorable event.

Such were the plantation days in old Waimanalo.

Bellows Air Force Station is another matter. Non-military visitors are limited to entering the reservation on weekends and holidays to enjoy the magnificent beach and camping areas. The beach is backed by a pleasant forest, and O'ahu residents rate Bellows Beach Park third for family fun.

BELLOWS AIR FORCE STATION

For thirty-seven years after the founding of Waimanalo Sugar Company the land now occupied by Bellows Air Force Station was planted in sugar cane. The Bellows lands made up perhaps one-fifth of the total cultivated by the sugar company.

By 1917 war had broken out in Europe, and the United States was anticipating joining the hostilities on the side of England and France. Something had to be done to strengthen O'ahu's defenses.

In February 1917 President Woodrow Wilson (1856-1924) transmitted an Executive Order to Territorial Governor Lucius E. Pinkham (1850-1922), setting aside some 1,500 acres of Waimanalo plantation's sugar lands to be known as Waimanalo Military Reservation. The security of O'ahu was advanced at the cost to Waimanalo Sugar Company of some 3,500 tons of raw sugar produced biennially on the lands surrendered. It was thought to be a small price to pay, considering that no enemy would attempt a landing at fortified Waimanalo Beach.

However, when it became clear that the war's center of hostilities would be confined to Europe, the Army stripped O'ahu of seasoned troops and sent them to France, and the Waimanalo Reservation was neglected for the duration.

A move was made to fortify the Waimanalo Reservation in the mid-1920s by constructing emplacements for two 240-mm howitzers about a mile inland from the beach. These large-caliber cannon would rain heavy projectiles on any enemy craft foolish enough to attempt a landing at Waimanalo Beach.

Infantry and artillery maneuvers occupied the reservation until about 1932 when a small airstrip was constructed running inland from the beach. Waimanalo Military Reservation then became a sub-post of Wheeler Field. In 1933, to signify the transformation to an Army Air Corps facility, the reservation was renamed Bellows Field in memory of 2nd Lt. Franklin Barney Bellows (1896-1918) who had been killed in action in France.

Bellows Field became an auxiliary field for gunnery practice by Wheeler's fighter pilots and a location for anti-aircraft target practice. The field was on caretaker status between training exercises and no permanent structures were built.

March 1941 marked the beginning of substantial build-up at Bellows. The 86th Observation Squadron was moved from Wheeler Field and based at Bellows Field, and became the first Army Air Corps squadron to call Bellows Field its home base. This made Bellows a first rank Army Air Field.

The scruffy Army tents that the men lived in were soon augmented with newly constructed two-story barracks. (These were arranged around a quadrangle in the jungle-like area now used by the Marines for training maneuvers. No trace remains of the barracks.) Recruits training for Air Corps duties filled out the garrison assigned to Bellows, and the population of Bellows grew to over 500 men.

On November 17, 1941 an O-47B observation plane piloted by 2nd Lt. Millard C. Shibley, Jr. crashed in Waimanalo Bay during takeoff. It was the first fatal crash at Bellows as Lieutenant Shibley and his observer were killed. The main gate entrance to Bellows Field, long-remembered but now gone (removed about 1988), was named Shibley Gate in his memory.

The little Bellows airstrip did not escape the cruel events of December 7, 1941. Twelve P-40 fighters were temporarily located at Bellows for gunnery practice when Japanese fighters swept down to strafe the field. There were only three pilots present that early Sunday morning but those three bravely rose to meet the challenge. 2nd Lt. Hans C. Christiansen was killed by a Japanese bullet as he climbed into his cockpit, 2nd Lt. George A. Whitman was shot down before gaining altitude, and Lt. Samuel W. Bishop got slightly airborne before being jumped by a Japanese Zero fighter that shot him down into Waimanalo Bay. Bishop was able to swim ashore despite a broken leg.

The excitement of the day was far from over. A B-17, one of twelve from California due at Hickam Field in the midst of the attack, crash-landed at the Bellows airstrip. The pilot, 1st Lt. Robert H. Richards, was forced to ground loop the large plane to avoid running it off the end of the runway and into the town of Waimanalo.

Then early the next morning a miniature Japanese submarine ran aground on the reef off Bellows beach. (A sign located on a tree next to the access road indicates where this submarine came ashore.) The sorry captain of the two-man crew, Ensign Kazuo Sakamaki,

B-17 bomber that crash landed at Bellows Field during the December 7, 1941 Japanese attack. Note tall chimney of the Waimanalo Sugar Company sugarmill in the right-center. *(15th ABW Historian's Office, Hickam AFB)*

survived and became the first Japanese prisoner taken during World War II. A Native Hawaiian, Cpl. David Akui of the 298th Infantry Regiment, played a leading role in the ensign's capture.

Bellows Field served out the war as a training and auxiliary field. At war's end Bellows Air Force Base (today Air Force Station) began a transition to an oasis for rest and recreation for off-duty personnel. Beach front cottages were built for enlisted, commissioned, and VIPs alike. The recreation facilities include tree-shaded camping areas, tennis courts, hiking trails, a driving range, a miniature golf course, restaurant and clubhouse facilities, a gas station and exchange and, of course, the magnificent Waimanalo Beach.

During weekends and holidays half of the beachfront area is opened to civilian use. The forested area next to the beach has become one of the most popular camping areas on O'ahu.

Midget Japanese submarine that ran ashore at Bellows beach the night of December 7, 1941. The submarine was supposed to enter Pearl Harbor but its steering gear went awry. Note Mokulua Island located off Lanikai in the background. *(15th ABW Historian's Office, Hickam AFB)*

CHAPTER THREE

WAIMANALO TO KAILUA

CASTLE HOSPITAL IS on the left across the intersection of Kalanianaole Highway with Kailua Road. To your right is a park with Castle Fountain. Who were these Castles, anyway? You will encounter the name repeatedly as you pass through Windward Oʻahu. The story of patriarch James Bicknell Castle is a piece of Oʻahu's history.

THE KING OF DEVELOPERS

It would have been impossible to predict the impact the descendents of Samuel Northrup Castle (1808-1894) would have on Oʻahu when he arrived in Honolulu in 1837 with the eighth company of American missionaries. Widowed in 1841, he returned to his native New York to marry his deceased wife's sister, Mary Tenney (1819-1907), then came back to Hawaiʻi to prosper as a business agent for the mission and, later, as a co-founder of the great mercantile firm, Castle & Cooke.

Samuel and Mary Castle had ten children and the sixth-born was James Bicknell Castle (1855-1918). By any standard he was the King of Developers of Windward Oʻahu.

Few people were born with more advantages than those enjoyed by the Castle children. By 1855 Castle & Cooke was a preeminent mercantile firm in Honolulu and James made the most of his advantageous position.

Following his graduation from Ohio's Oberlin College, James led a gentleman's life for a time. He met and married Julia White (1849-1943) during a leisurely European tour. Returning to Honolulu he joined his father's firm and became a partner in 1886. His entrepreneurial bent began to make its appearance during this time and he was far too imaginative and ambitious for staid and established Castle & Cooke.

He was determined to use his fortune to further the betterment of Hawai'i. It became his habit to choose and develop an area somewhere in the islands, and, having seen the enterprise succeed, sell it off to raise capital for his next endeavor.

James left Castle & Cooke 1889 to strike out on his own. He had a grand scheme to develop Windward O'ahu, from Kahuku south to Kailua, as one vast agricultural domain, mostly in sugarcane and ranching.

His first move was in 1890 when, with his friend and fellow missionary son Lorrin Thurston (1858-1931) and others, he formed Kahuku Plantation Company on lands subleased from Benjamin F. Dillingham (1844-1918). The plantation anchored the northern end of his development plans. In 1896 the Kahuku company made a deal to mill the cane grown to the south on the Mormon Church's Laie Plantation, effectively increasing Castle-controlled sugarcane acreage by some 2,000 acres.

Castle now turned to the southern end of his grand scheme. He had in mind to connect the terminus of Dillingham's Oahu Railway

James Bicknell Castle (1855-1918) and Julia White Castle (1849-1943). *(Bishop Museum)*

& Land Company (O.R.& L.) in Kahuku with the proposed street railway system in Honolulu by building a railroad along the Windward Coast. Lorrin Thurston had started the Honolulu Rapid Transit & Land Company and the company was running short of money before beginning operations. In 1901 Castle persuaded his brother, William, and his father's estate to come to the rescue and put money into the company through purchase of controlling shares of the transit company's stock.

In 1898 Castle's energies were distracted from his development plans when he became a partner in Alexander & Baldwin. However, by 1905 he was able to return to his plans for Windward O'ahu when he founded the Koolau Railroad Company. Eventually this railroad was built from Kahuku as far south as Kahana Bay.

Now it was time to flesh out his agricultural domain. In 1907 he bought shares in the vast Kaneohe Ranch Company, eventually owning all of it. This added 7,000 acres of land in Kailua and Kane'ohe to Castle's holdings.

Next, in 1909, Castle formed the Koolau Agricultural Company that purchased the land south of La'ie to Kahana Bay. He planted sugarcane and used his railroad to haul the harvested cane to the Kahuku mill.

Castle envisioned adding to his Kane'ohe Ranch holdings by revitalizing the Heeia Agricultural Company plantation that had closed down in 1902. Concurrently, his plan was to extend his Koolau Railroad Company south from Kahana Bay, through Kane'ohe and Kailua, and on to Waimanalo where it would pass through a tunnel into Manoa Valley and connect with his partially-owned Honolulu Rapid Transit & Land Company street railway.

His development plans were vast and grand but James Bicknell Castle died in 1918 before he was able to complete them. His railroad never got further south than Kahana Bay, eventually stopped passenger service in 1933, and had closed down entirely by 1952.

James and Julia White Castle had one child, Harold Kainalu Long Castle (1886-1967), who carried on in his father's tradition. Using his inheritance, he implemented many worthy works in Windward O'ahu.

In a 1956 interview Harold Castle revealed something of his guiding philosophy regarding the use of the Castle lands. "Why," his interviewer asked, "did you sell that golf course land at the bottom of the Pali [Pali Public Golf Course] for $225,000 when it's worth more [far more] than a million dollars now?"

"I just wanted to," Harold replied. "When you come over the Pali and see the grandeur and beauty of this section of the island—well I couldn't visualize the area used for, say, a low-cost housing project. It would have ruined it forever."

Harold K. L. Castle perpetuated his father's public-spirited stewardship when disposing parts of the Ranch's lands. Chief among the gifts were parcels for Castle High School, Kainalu Elementary School in Kailua, and the land occupied by Central Union Windward Church. Later charitable giving by Castle interests included the land and much of the costs of Castle Hospital, and the campus occupied by the Windward Branch of Hawaii Pacific University.

While driving towards the ocean on Kailua Road you will catch glimpses of a large expanse of wetlands on the left side of the road. This is Kawainui Marsh, the largest freshwater wetland in Hawai'i. The story of this marsh is part of the history of the *ahupua'a* of Kailua.

KAWAINUI MARSH

Over one thousand years before Columbus crossed the Atlantic to discover America for Europeans, some unknown Polynesians navigated 2,400 miles of Pacific Ocean from the Marquesas to discover Hawai'i for themselves. The exact date is unknown, but it is believed that the first Polynesian landfall on Hawai'i took place sometime between 200 A.D. and 400 A.D. The first settlements were scattered throughout the islands in locations hospitable to subsistence living. One such location for the earliest of the settlements was at the edges of Kailua's magnificent Kawainui Marsh.

Difficult as it is to imagine today, the area was a lagoon at the time of the earliest settlements. The entrance was protected by a coral reef. The coral mound surmounted with a banyan tree that fronts the Windward Passage condominium in Kailua is a remnant of this reef. Between 200 to 400 A.D. and 1600 A.D. the ocean tides brought in bottom sand to fill in and around this reef to form the land now occupied by Kailua town, making modern-day changes to the shoreline of Kailua Bay look like child's play.

Radiocarbon dating of charcoal deposits indicate that human activity took place near the lagoon as early as the fifth century. The slender archeological evidence suggests that agricultural activities predominated. The nature of the activities changed after the lagoon's entrance filled in and Kawainui became an inland pond. Its waters were fed by the runoff from mountain steams and freshets and the pond became more hospitable to fish and fowl.

The Hawaiians stocked it with fish and periodically cleaned it of grass and detritus. Legend has it that the pond was protected by the goddess Luawahine. The Hawaiians were grateful for the reliable and rich harvests and showed their devotions by constructing two large *heiau* (temples) nearby. Both survive. Ulupo Heiau is an official State Monument and is located next to Kailua Road adjacent to the YMCA. Pahukini Heiau, located upland of the former Kapa'a landfill, has been restored in recent years and can be visited.

There can be little doubt that Kawainui Marsh was a pond at the time of the discovery of the islands by English Capt. James Cook (1728-1779). Legends originating before Cook's time tell of the abundant fishing in Kawainui. The Hawaiian historian Samuel

View of Kawainui Marsh. This marsh is the largest freshwater marsh in the state. Native Hawaiians once stocked the interior pond with fish. The Coconut Grove section of Kailua is at the left border and Maunawili is in the right distance of this photograph. *(W. H. Dorrance)*

Kamakau (1815-1876) described how Kamehameha I showed his common touch by working in the fishpond of Kawainui in the years around 1804.

With the decline of Hawaiian population the pond was abandoned to the grasses and became marsh land. In the latter part of the nineteenth-century Chinese planters took over the many terraces toward Maunawili, and an era of rice-growing displaced Hawaiian agriculture and pond use. Cattle grazing added to the marsh's pollution. Sugarcane planting in Waimanalo and the region surrounding Kaelepulu Pond began after the Waimanalo Sugar Company was organized in 1878.

In 1925 the Waimanalo Sugar Company began tapping the marsh for irrigation water. A large pump lifted marsh water some 340 feet up Mount Olomana into a tunnel that drained the water down to the Waimanalo side and into an irrigation reservoir.

Little more was done that affected the marsh until after World War II. Kailua town was blossoming and the area east of, and bordering, the marsh and known as Coconut Grove began to fill with housing. The area was a flood plain when the marsh overflowed, as it did after a rare, sustained torrential downpour. Developers pressed for a solution to insure the land never flooded.

The Flood Control Act of 1950 authorized the Army Corps of Engineers to dredge a channel and build a levee bordering the marsh. The Corps was to do the work with costs shared by the federal and territorial governments. Work began in 1964 after years of marking time while awaiting appropriations. The Corps dredged the Oneawa Channel and silt basin, and built a levee and groin along the eastern edge of the marsh. At last, in June 1966 the work was done and a dedication ceremony held attended by the grateful populace.

An awareness of the historical importance of the marsh developed, driven by knowledgeable residents of the area. In 1983 the concerns coalesced in the establishment of the non-profit Kawai Nui Heritage Foundation as an outgrowth of a committee formed years earlier by the Lani-Kailua Outdoor Circle. The foundation is dedicated to the preservation of the marsh and educating the citizenry as to its rich history.

On December 31, 1987-January 1, 1988 disaster struck in the form of a "100-year flood" brought on by a lengthy, torrential rain. The levee overflowed and millions of dollars in damage were inflicted on homes that were flooded in Coconut Grove. In 1993 a Corps of Engineers' plan to heighten the levee was approved by the City Council, and $10.4 million of federal funds were allocated to the job. The earthen levee was raised by 4-1/2 feet, topped with a 4 foot high concrete barrier. A walk along this levee provides an excellent view of the marsh and the Koʻolau Pali.

The State Department of Land and Natural Resources is working on a master plan for the marsh which will become a state park and recreational facility. As with any such community effort, the words and suggestions are many, conflicts develop, and compromises are made. Out of it will come an enhanced awareness of the beautiful asset that has lain dormant and been taken for granted all these years. The heritage of the state's largest freshwater wetland will be preserved.

Kailua was reported to have a population of 36,818 in the 1990 census. Nevertheless, Kailua was hardly a town within the memories of elderly residents.

OLD KAILUA TOWN

Kailua didn't exist as a town in 1915. The road from Honolulu over the Pali was steep and twisting. The road to Kailua from the junction of the road now called Kalanianaole Highway with the Pali Road was rutted and unpaved. Potable water was obtained from a spring at the foot of Ulupo Heiau. Very few people lived in Kailua.

However, there were visionaries who saw possibilities in the location. By 1917 prominent *kama'aina* and missionary descendent Arthur Hyde Rice (1878-1953), scion of the Kaua'i sugar-planting Rice family, had built a successful Honolulu brokerage firm and longed for the life and surroundings of his Kaua'i youth. He approached equally-prominent missionary descendent Harold K. L. Castle, and purchased some 350 acres of Kailua *ahupua'a* in the location now known as Coconut Grove. He built a spacious home within the parcel and lived there the remainder of his life. Thirty years would pass before Coconut Grove filled with homes.

Harold Castle's Kaneohe Ranch Company leased out much of the land in Kailua to small-parcel farmers, many of them Japanese. A Japanese language school was started in 1919 at the present-day location of the Kailua Library. It was one of very few structures in Kailua at the time.

Finally, in 1921, the road to Kailua from the junction of the Pali Road and the road now called Kalanianaole Highway was paved. Arthur Rice subdivided his Coconut Grove holdings and put the lots up for sale.

By 1924 Kailua was sparsely occupied. The Kailua Tavern, located at the corner of today's Kuulei Road and Oneawa Street and now occupied by a Shell service station, had recently opened and served as a landmark. Few of the lots in Coconut Grove had been sold. Kailua was just too remote from busy Honolulu to attract buyers.

In 1924, Charles R. Frazier and some associates purchased the land in Lanikai, subdivided it into lots, paved the streets, and offered the lots for sale. Such was the identity of Frazier's new community in Kailua that until 1958 the post office in Kailua was called "Lanikai" because using "Kailua" would cause confusion with the Kailua-Kona post office on the Big Island of Hawai'i.

There were only two grocery stores serving Kailua in the 1920s. Both were near where Castle Hospital is now located; Matsuda's Store and Kodama's Store. The area near them was farmed by small-parcel tenant farmers who grew much of the fresh produce sold in the stores.

Until 1929, when the elementary school moved to its present location, the only elementary school in Kailua *ahupua'a* was located in Maunawili. This one-room school, presided over by Mr. Akuni Ahau, was located near the present-day intersection of the Pali Highway and Maunawili Road. For a time a rice mill operated across the road from the school and water buffalo worked the adjacent rice paddies.

Solomon Kalapawai Mahoe, Jr. (b. 1913) told of attending this school and of serving later as a beachboy at Waikiki Beach. His experiences tell much of old Kailua. It seems that when the Kailua Tavern was open for business in the evening a lantern would be hoisted that could be seen from afar. When Waikiki beachboy Solomon and colleagues, accompanied by young women, planned to visit the tavern they drove to the Pali lookout. They went to the tavern if they saw the lantern. If not, they returned to Waikiki.

Dairy farming came to Kailua in a big way in 1924 when Mr. and Mrs. Lawrence Campos moved their operation to Kailua. The lands now occupied by numerous enterprises including the former Consumer Tire warehouse, Daiei Mart, Safeway, apartment complexes, and Windward Passage condominiums were leased from Kaneohe Ranch and converted to pasture land for Campos Dairy. This operation grew to over a thousand head of cattle before closing down in the 1960s.

In 1936 Harold Castle opened Kalama subdivision, calling it the "Land of Enchantment." He put in roads and water mains and subdivided it into 186 lots. A buyer got membership in the Kalama Beach Club with the purchase. The Kailua Racquet Club opened in 1937 surrounded by resident lots.

Mrs. Juliet Magoon opened the Kailua Theater in 1938 on Kailua Road where the Goodyear Tire store is now located. Residents of the community no longer had to travel to Waimanalo or Kane'ohe to see a movie. Date's Flying A service station moved from Waimanalo to the corner of Kailua Road and Oneawa Street that same year.

Kailua's sporting blood enjoyed Saturday and Sunday outings at the Kailua Racetrack from 1938 till 1947. It was located on and near the grounds of today's Kainalu Elementary School. A Japanese farmer raised watermelons on the infield.

The first pharmacy came to Kailua in 1942 when Mr. Francis Hughes rented space in a corner of the Kailua Tavern and put up partitions "to avoid drinkers." Eventually Hughes expanded to three locations before he sold out in 1974.

In 1947 Alice Davis and Eleanor N. Vogel opened the Davis Building, Kailua's first office building, on land leased from Kaneohe Ranch Company, and located at the corner of Kailua Road and today's Hamakua Drive. Another welcome addition was built in 1948 when the Kailua Library opened on the former location of the Japanese language school, next to Kailua Elementary School.

In a 1974 interview Francis Hughes listed the following enterprises as existing in Kailua in the 1940s and 1950s: Liberty House (first a small shop, replaced with present large store), Harada's store (gone), Tom Date service station (gone), Lanikai store (gone), Kalapawai Market (founded in 1932 and still there), Kam family market (gone), Tomasa's (gone), Charlie's Sportswear (gone), Kanetake's (still going), Kailua Theater (gone), Rocky's liquor (gone), and Governor John Burns liquor (gone). As can be seen, most of these enterprises are now history. By 1955 the population in and around Kailua had grown to over 5,000 and Kailua was changing from a rural and beachfront community to the bedroom community it is today. Old Kailua has passed from the O'ahu scene.

❖   ❖   ❖

Kailua Beach, a broad 2-3/4 mile crescent of sand lined with trees and residences, has long been rated among the very best in the United States. In the recent (1997) survey, Oʻahu residents rated Kailua Beach third for snorkeling and swimming, second for sunning and viewing, and second for family fun, the only beach on Oʻahu to be

Kailua Beach as viewed from ʻAlala Point at the Lanikai end of the beach. The dark structure in the left center is the boat launching ramp much used by local fishermen. (W. H. Dorrance)

ranked in the top five in all three categories. (Waikiki Beach, for example, was rated first for sunning and viewing and fifth for family fun by the local residents.) And those aren't the only activities at Kailua Beach. Surfing, kayaking, canoeing, and sailboarding are other popular pursuits. Kailua Beach is a public beach available to all comers, as are all beaches on Oʻahu.

A short stretch of winding and rising road takes you around a bend into the cul-de-sac roads serving the community known as Lanikai. It is hemmed in by Kaʻiwa Ridge on the right and enjoys a rich history of its own.

LANIKAI

Turkeys roaming the Kaʻiwa Ridge foothills on Poʻo Poʻo Place in exclusive Lanikai! It couldn't be. Those houses bring upwards of a million dollars in today's market. But pre-1924, there was no community called "Lanikai" and turkeys had a legitimate claim to scratch the earth among the watermelon patches. Turkeys, watermelons, and a fishing shack near the shore, periodically used by owner Harold K. L. Castle, were all that distinguished what is now known as Lanikai back then as Harold Castle said in a 1957 interview.

Prominent *kama'aina* Erling W. Hedemann, Jr., in a 1978 interview, told of his father taking him to the beach near Harold Castle's rudimentary canoe house where they fished for *ulua* (jack or tuna) offshore. It was about 1924, he remembered, or maybe a year or two earlier.

Hedemann's father bought a small lot, erected an old Army tent that was locked in a shed when not in use, and created a weekend oasis away from their home in Honolulu. In a couple of years the tent was replaced with a modest beach house but things were still pretty primitive. There was no running water or electricity and today's Mokulua and Aalapapa Drives did not exist. Kerosene lanterns supplied the light, and drinking water was imported in jugs. Standard Oil Company did a good business supplying kerosene to residents of Windward O'ahu.

Kailua Beach at the Lanikai end. The unusual house high on the bluff above 'Alala Point marks the entrance to Lanikai. The boat launching ramp is located between the beached canoes and the shore below the point. *(W. H. Dorrance)*

Hedemann spent many pleasant childhood days at this weekend hideaway. Sea turtles were prolific and the net he and his father set might bring a harvest of one hundred fish during *moi* (threadfin fish) season. Hedemann's younger sister often brought in a lobster caught at the coral outcroppings offshore and his mother would cook it for lunch. The glass balls that were used to suspend deep sea fishermen's nets drifted ashore in abundance. Hedemann recalled that his record collection for one morning was thirty-three glass balls.

Even the swarms of mosquitoes failed to dampen their enthusiasm. Flit guns and mosquito netting kept an uneasy truce. The kids ignored the pests and the adults did their best to keep them away, with little success. Mosquitoes were a problem until they had an eradication program years later.

Today's Lanikai community with the Mokulua Islands located offshore. Photo taken from crest of Ka'iwa Ridge. Two World War II fire control stations are located on this ridge. *(W. H. Dorrance)*

In those early days there was no Kailua town, no post office, no shopping centers, no service stations, no paved roads, and no "Lanikai.". The closest store was Matsuda's located on what was then a winding, unpaved, and rutted road that led from the Pali to Kailua Beach. Closer to the beach along this road was Ulupo Heiau. Behind the *heiau,* on the Kawainui Marsh side, was a clear water spring (still there) that served as the source of potable water for thirsty residents. It was country.

While Erling Hedemann, Jr. was enjoying this childhood, Charles R. Frazier was bringing his decade-long skirmish with the Outdoor Circle to an end. Advertising man Frazier owned the largest outdoor billboard company, Pioneer Advertising Company, and his large billboards drew the ire of the ladies of Outdoor Circle. It was an unequal struggle. While Frazier was able to hold the Circle off for over ten years, by 1926 he was ready to throw in the towel, and sold out to a fund raised by the Outdoor Circle. We have them to thank for permanently removing the visual billboard blight from O'ahu.

By then Frazier's energies were directed elsewhere. He knew that big plans were afoot to exploit the growing post-World War I tourist trade. Matson Navigation Company planned to build a luxury hotel (later named the Royal Hawaiian) at Waikiki Beach, to be occupied by prosperous tourists from the mainland. An equally-luxurious steamer, *Malolo,* was being built to transport affluent visitors to O'ahu. Frazier saw it as a business opportunity.

He reasoned that visitors prosperous enough to afford the fares of the luxurious *Malolo* and a stay at the new Royal Hawaiian Hotel would probably be prosperous enough to buy land and build a house in an exclusive community on O'ahu. After all, a certain number of the visitors couldn't fail to see the merits to living on O'ahu, especially if advertising man Frazier made it clear on terms that would appeal to them.

In 1924 Frazier assembled a small number of O'ahu investors with himself as principal and purchased two large parcels, one from Helene Irwin Fagan and the other from Harold K.L. Castle, that he intended to develop into a community he would call "Lanikai" in the mistaken belief it meant "heavenly sea." (It was close. In Hawaiian it means "sea heaven.")

Frazier described his development in an elaborate brochure that drew on the skills of his advertising agency. To enhance the attraction of Lanikai, his group leased an additional 185 acres of Bishop Estate land between Ka'iwa Ridge and Kaelepulu Stream for a golf course that he called "Kailua Country Club" (now, Mid-Pacific Country Club), designed by prominent golf course architect Seth Raynor. The group laid out a loop of roads in "Lanikai, Crescent of Content," paved them, and divided the land into lots that were promptly put up for sale through agent Trent Trust Company. Just to make it clear as to who was eligible to purchase the lots his brochure stated: "Considering the character of those who already have bought at Lanikai, it is clear this will be a closely-knit, harmonious, neighborly community of well-to-do people."

In 1925 the cylindrical stone column marking the entrance to Lanikai was erected and several lots had been sold, mostly to O'ahu residents. That same year the City and County of Honolulu installed a water system and development accelerated. The community filled with a mixture of long-time O'ahu residents, privacy-seeking movie and theatrical performers and artists, and affluent mainlanders. A first-generation of beach houses lined Lanikai Beach and substantial homes were built in the foothills of

Kaʻiwa Ridge. Lanikai was the first residential development on Windward Oʻahu.

A small store, presided over by Mr. and Mrs. Akai, opened nearby on Kailua Road close to the beach. The first Kailua post office was located inside and the postal address was "Lanikai" for all residents in the vicinity.

World War II brought excitement to Lanikai when the military used the Mokulua Islands as bombing targets. Today the beach houses are largely second and third-generation, prices have increased, and few lots are vacant. Charles Russell Frazier's dream community has matured into the neighborly suburb that he envisioned in his brochure.

As you round the point on Alala Road to enter Lanikai, a curious structure high on this ridge catches the eye. It's not a house. In fact, it's not a "pillbox," either. It is a fire control station constructed during the war year of 1942. This station, and a similar one on the ridge closer to Bellows Field, housed optical instruments (the pedestals for the instruments are still there) used by the coast artillery to determine target positions for large-caliber cannons emplaced around the island.

World War II Coast Artillery fire control station located above Lanikai on Kaʻiwa Ridge. Note Lanikai below, Popoiʻa Island (Flat Island) in the left center, and Ulupaʻu Crater on Mokapu Peninsula in the upper left. *(W. H. Dorrance)*

A climb to this station is quite rewarding. The climb is a little more arduous than the Diamond Head Lookout climb, without helpful stairs along the way, but the views from the 580-foot crest rival those at Diamond Head. Be sure to wear proper hiking shoes and garb if you undertake this climb, however. Do not attempt the climb in or immediately after rainy weather! The muddy trail becomes very slippery when wet.

The trailhead is located off to the side of a private driveway that leads up the hill from Kaelepulu Drive just before the gates of the Bluestone townhouse community.

On the slopes of Ka'iwa Ridge, the lots between Aalapapa and Mokulua, and the lots along the shore on the ocean side of Mokulua are almost totally occupied with residences, many of them quite substantial. The first-time visitor is often at a loss to determine the location of the famous Lanikai Beach because of this. As recently as 1996 it was recognized as the best in the United States and the recent poll of O'ahu residents rated it fifth on the island for snorkeling and swimming.

Lanikai has long been a favorite retreat for performers in the arts, prominent island residents, and interesting active and retired professionals in general.

LANIKAI LADY

Marsue McGinnis had just graduated from Ohio's Miami University with a degree in education in the spring of 1945, and had a romantic notion of seeing the world by teaching. A notice from the Territory of Hawaii had circulated among midwestern colleges seeking newly-graduated teachers. Marsue applied and was accepted. The last week in August, 1945 found her in San Francisco embarking on the liner *Matsonia* bound for Honolulu. The war in the Pacific was not yet officially ended and the *Matsonia* was fitted out as a troop transport. Marsue's fellow passengers included soldiers and many young people returning to their homes in the islands after spending the war years at school on the mainland.

Marsue was assigned to a school in Laupahoehoe on the Big Island of Hawai'i. She took her very first air trip to Hilo on an inter-island plane. There she and six other young teachers bound for schools on the north Hilo and Hamakua coasts were met with two cars that would take them to their destinations.

The trip north on the winding and narrow government road was filled with beauty. The road twisted and turned while dipping into and around gulches under a canopy of tropical trees. Here and there were glimpses of the ocean. It was a far cry from the scenes of the Midwest. Marsue was enchanted.

After two hours or so the car pulled up in front of a magnificent house in Pepeʻekeo. The plantation manager had tea and lunch served in honor of the new teachers. The large dining room was resplendent with oriental carpeting, and a table set with crystal, silver, and fine linens. "This is a fine life that I'm joining", thought Marsue, as the hostesses and guests seated themselves around the room.

Then she was startled by a large cockroach ambling across the carpet. Her view of things began to change. She was indeed seeing the world.

Following lunch the young teachers were driven to their destination in Laupahoehoe. Four of them, including Marsue, were to be housed in a cottage located on low-lying Laupahoehoe peninsula near the shore. The setting was breathtaking; in one direction the Pacific Ocean, in the opposite were sea cliffs topped with green cane fields, snow-topped Mauna Kea looming in the distance. She had never imagined living in such beautiful surroundings.

The young teachers made themselves at home and took up their assignments. The community was pleased that the school had a full staff again after the wartime shortage. Then cruel disaster struck.

On the morning of April 1, 1946 a deadly series of tidal waves hit Hawaiʻi. Nobody was prepared for it, least of all the young teachers and students on Laupahoehoe Peninsula. It was devastating. While there was time to reach high ground, had they known of the danger, three huge waves washed over the peninsula before the native Hawaiian residents, teachers, and early-arriving students could run to safety.

Many were washed to sea in a tangle of rubble. Three of the four teachers from Marsue's cottage, other teachers, several students, and native Hawaiian family members, a total of thirty-two, drowned in the raging waters. A terrified Marsue clung to a floating door as she was washed further offshore.

Marsue was certain the world had ended. There had been no warning of this. Then she made out people waving and moving on the seaside cliffs that line the Hamakua Coast. There was hope, but most of the day passed without a rescuer. She didn't want to wash up against the rocky cliffs. Maybe, she thought, she would float ashore at O'okala where there was a landing. Maybe.

She spotted a head in the swells a few yards away. It was a young man who was clinging to flotsam. They shouted encouragement to each other. Where were the boats? They caught sight of an inter-island steamer further out that was south-bound to Hilo. The boy shouted that he was going to swim to the ship. "It's too far!" shouted Marsue. The boy struck out toward the steamer.

He was never seen again.

There was desperation on shore. Every boat on the windward coast of Hawai'i had been lost in the tsunami, even those in Hilo. Finally one was located, and a truck was sent to fetch it. At last the boat arrived but was found to be unsuitable for mounting an outboard motor.

Plantation carpenters frantically went to work. They never did a better job or worked faster. They squared off the end of the boat, attached a new stern, and mounted the motor. Four men, the plantation physician, the owner of the motor, a scuba diver, and a Native Hawaiian who knew the ocean, shoved off in search of survivors. It had been over ten hours since the tsunami first struck.

The rescue boat pulled two young boys out of the water. There had to be more. Finally a rescue plane dropped an inflatable raft near Marsue. She pulled the cord that inflated the raft and climbed aboard. Within minutes the rescue boat spotted her perched on the raft. Rescue at last! It was the doctor who helped lift an exhausted Marsue into the boat.

It had been an exciting year for the young teacher but her story doesn't end here. Marsue and the doctor who rescued her were married before the year was out. She continued teaching for a year and then retired to become a housewife and mother of the doctor's two young children from a previous marriage. Now Marsue began to see yet another side of the world as a doctor's wife.

Three plantation hospitals were served by her husband with the largest one at Papa'aloa next to Laupahoehoe. Marsue and her family lived near this hospital. She still marvels at the wonderful efficiency with which the staff served the plantation residents.

"Frequently I see a distorted description of plantation life in the papers," says Marsue, now the widow McShane. "It wasn't the way it's described at all. The houses were neat, comfortable and all had running water and electricity. The schools were good, maybe better than they are now. And the medical care was excellent, just the best. Each of the three hospitals had nurses on staff who went out to visit every family. They brought in persons who needed the doctor's attention if the patient didn't come in of his or her own accord. I saw it all and I can tell you that people lived very well in those plantation villages.

"The union fixed up the wages but there was no need to fix up the medical care and housing. And, until the tsunami wiped out the railroad, everybody had a convenient way to go to shop in Hilo. The trains ran on schedule and everybody used them. It was a real disappointment when the tsunami shut the railroad down. It was a good life."

CHAPTER FOUR

KAILUA TO PALI LOOKOUT

MAUNAWILI

THE PICTURESQUE SETTLEMENT of Maunawili is located in the *ahupuaʻa* of Kailua and tucked away in a lush valley between the Koʻolau Range and Mount Olomana. The location was populated by native Hawaiians long before Capt. James Cook made his voyage of discovery. The region was heavily terraced for *taro* patches and kept green by frequent rains and the runoff of mountain water. Four mountain streams combined with Maunawili Stream to carry fresh water down to Kaiwainui Marsh (then a pond). Kailua *ahupuaʻa* was one of the most desirable locations on Oʻahu because of the Maunawili *taro* patches and the fish in Kawainui Pond.

Map showing location of Maunawili community relative to Kailua and the Pali Highway. (W. H. Dorrance)

Two *heiau*, Halaualolo and Kukapoki, were located in Maunawili and their locations are given on today's maps. Their proximity to each other is testimony to the comparatively dense native population in Maunawili Valley in ancient times.

Capt. John Harbottle (unk.-1830) was an English seafaring man who settled on Oʻahu in 1793. He was one of very few *haole* (white person) on Oʻahu at that time, and soon made himself useful to King Kamehameha I as a sea captain and navigator. Harbottle settled down in Honolulu with a high-born Hawaiian wife and the king awarded him land on which to make his home.

Mr. and Mrs. Harbottle had several attractive daughters. Robert Boyd, a humble ship's carpenter, was among Harbottle's small circle of English expatriate contemporaries. Boyd married one of Harbottle's daughters and settled on land in Honolulu awarded by the king. A son, James H. Boyd, was born of this marriage. When James H. Boyd married it was to have implications for Maunawili.

Mr. and Mrs. James H. Boyd prospered, and by the early 1870s the family had a spacious home in Maunawili. It became known for lavish *luʻau* and entertainment of royalty, writers, artists, and dignitaries visiting Oʻahu. The Boyds were close friends of the monarchy.

In April 1877 Lydia Liliʻuokalani (1839-1917), sister of King David Kalakaua, was named heir apparent to the throne. Princess Liliʻuokalani made plans to tour the islands with her husband John O. Dominis (1832-1891), governor of Oʻahu. As told in her biography, they spent the first night of the tour at the country home of Mr. and Mrs. J. H. Boyd in Maunawili. The visit made a lasting impression on the princess.

Liliʻuokalani was a talented composer. She composed the haunting melody "Aloha Oe" that serves as a farewell to visitors departing from Hawaiʻi. The inscription "Maunawili 1877" in Liliʻuokalani's handwriting appears on the border of the original score.

In 1880 King Kalakaua selected James H. Boyd's son Robert N. Boyd, a Punahou School student, as one of three scholars to be sent to Italy for a classic European education. It was the king's intent that the three return to serve in the Hawaiian government. Young Boyd's father, Col. James H. Boyd, served as Queen Liliʻuokalani's aide-de-camp when she ascended to the throne following King Kalakaua's death in 1891.

Several native Hawaiian residents of Maunawili gained free title to their *kuleana* (small land parcels) in the Great Mahele (land grants) of 1848-1850. Terraces of *taro,* banana plants, and the grass houses of the families were scattered throughout the valley. Most of the Hawaiians gave up their holdings to be replaced with Chinese rice farmers in the last decades of the nineteenth century. A rice mill was built near the present-day intersection of Maunawili and Auloa Roads and the Chinese prevailed until the 1920s when rice growing became unprofitable.

Former Maunawili resident Solomon Mahoe, Jr. recalled in a 1977 interview that only three native Hawaiian families remained living in Maunawili by 1930.

A new enterprise moved in about the time that the last of the rice planters departed. The Hawaiian Sugar Planters' Association (HSPA) breeding station was established in Maunawili in 1925. The station, now affiliated with the Hawaii Agriculture Research Center, successor to the HSPA, occupies acreage deep in Maunawili Valley at the very end of the paved section of Maunawili Road and plays an important role in Hawaiian agriculture.

Sugar was king when the Maunawili station, HSPA's second, was established. The location was chosen because Maunawili's climate duplicates that of sugar cultivation regions on Hawai'i's sugar islands. Several new strains of sugarcane have been produced here. The search for insect, disease, rodent, and rot-resistant strains of sugarcane continues. It is doubtful that the sugar industry could have survived so long without the hundreds of new strains produced at the Maunawili breeding station. Recently it was announced that the station would broaden its research into alternate crops for Hawai'i.

For years Honolulu-bound and Kailua-bound commuters were treated to the sight of a water buffalo wallowing in the mud flats of Maunawili Stream next to the Pali Road. It ended in 1960 when the "unofficial mayor of Maunawili," Moses Salinas, was forced to give up his banana farm because of old age.

Today much of Maunawili is a quiet residential community that doubles as a suburb of Kailua town and a place to call home for many a retiree and Honolulu-bound worker.

An exclusive Japanese-owned golf course and club opened in Maunawili in 1993. Now in private hands and called "Luana Hills," the course is a challenge for golfers, located as it is on the flanks of Mount Olomana. Few of the members resided on O'ahu until the ownership changed hands. One of Hawai'i's most beautiful locations had been turned over to the private pursuits of wealthy Japanese. When the ownership changed hands, this pleasant location became available to all who could afford the green fees.

THE OLD PALI ROAD

The island of O'ahu was formed two to three million years ago by eruptions of two adjacent volcanoes. The erosion caused by the rise and fall of the ocean has worn away the seaside edges of the volcanic craters so that two curved mountain ranges remain—the western Wai'anae range and the eastern Ko'olau range. In order to travel from Honolulu to Windward O'ahu one must cross over or go around the Ko'olaus.

Crossing over was the most direct route, yet it was a challenge to the ancient Hawaiians. They would climb up the walls of the escarpment to reach a pass leading to Nu'uanu Valley's gentle slopes falling to Honolulu. For centuries, Hawaiians took their produce to the Honolulu side by this climb.

Westerners imported horses to the islands beginning in 1803. The crude footpaths and hand holds down the face of the pali were not sufficient for horse travel. Until a gentler and wider road was constructed, the fertile lands of the windward side would remain in relative isolation.

This situation was intolerable to ambitious merchants and planters, so between 1830 and 1893 a succession of efforts converted the hazardous 800-foot climb to a six-foot wide path carved into the side of the *pali*. Rock falls and erosion made continuous repairs and maintenance of this primitive road necessary. The mountainside road builders had gone as far as pick and shovel would take them.

This first Pali Road was a terrible bottleneck. On the one hand the planters were expanding their cane and produce operations on the rich windward lands. On the other hand, the lack of a safe road limited the planters' access to the Honolulu markets and wharves. Pressures built to improve the Pali Road.

By 1893 the monarchy was deposed and Hawai'i became a republic, soon to be annexed to the United States. In that turbulent time a government-funded effort to improve the road was launched when the government appropriated the then magnificent sum of $40,000 to improve the Pali Road "once and for all."

Young Honolulu-born Stanford University engineering student John H. Wilson (1861-1956) teamed up with more experienced Lou M. Whitehead to submit a bid. Their bid of $37,500 won the award so they assembled a team of workmen, and in 1897 began the construction of a new road.

The road hewed by the team hugged the twists and turns of the mountainside. Tons of blasting powder were used to carve out a road designed for no more than an eight percent grade and widened to 20 feet in the process. It was the descent from the Pali Lookout down the windward face of the escarpment that presented the greatest challenge to the road builders. A sharp drop of 800 feet was involved.

A surviving section of the Old Pali Road that was constructed in 1898. It is possible to hike down to and beyond this segment of the road from the Pali Lookout. *(W. H. Dorrance)*

Wilson carved out a roadbed and, where that wasn't feasible, mounted the road on concrete shelving jutting out from the mountainside.

Johnny Wilson's old Pali Road served for some 55 years after it was opened in late 1897. Over the years sharper curves were lessened a little and other improvements made but the basic road remained as Wilson's and Whitehead's men built it.

The remnants of the road provide some of the most outstanding vistas on O'ahu. At the crest, the location of the present-day Pali Lookout, you command a view of the entire seaward Ko'olau plains and the Pacific Ocean beyond it.

It was at this crest that Kamehameha I fought the last battle that won dominion for him over the island of O'ahu. Here, in 1795, Kamehameha's warriors defeated the forces of the Kalanikupule (1760-

View of Kane'ohe *ahupua'a* from the Pali Lookout. The open area in the center is the Hawaiian Memorial Park Cemetery. Kualoa Park at the head of Kane'ohe Bay is at the upper left edge. *(W. H. Dorrance)*

1795), then the ruling chief of O'ahu. Hundreds of Kalanikupule's followers, men, women and children, were driven over this cliff. There can be no doubt of the nature of the climax of the battle. Wilson's and Whitehead's construction workers found over three hundred skulls at the foot of the Old Pali Road.

By 1955 the road was in need of major repair and complaints were growing. Modern-road building equipment was now available, and strategically-placed tunnels could straighten out the road and reduce grades. Money was appropriated by the Territory and bids were solicited for the construction of a new Pali Road.

Work began on the new and present-day Pali Road in March 1955. Four tunnels were dug through the mountains making the new road somewhat lower and straighter, and separate lanes were constructed for Honolulu-bound and Windward-bound drivers. On 11 May 1957 the new Pali Road was complete. The commute from the Windward side to Honolulu could no longer be described as a minor adventure.

And what of the remaining years of young engineer Johnny Wilson?

John Henry Wilson possessed a distinguished Hawaiian lineage. His father, Charles B. Wilson, half-Tahitian and half-British, was Queen Lili'uokalani's loyal marshal. His mother was half-Tahitian and a confidante of the queen. John spoke fluent Hawaiian and was educated at the Royal School before attending Stanford University.

Wilson entered public service in 1907. He served in various engineering roles on Maui and then O'ahu. He was appointed Mayor of Honolulu in 1919 and won election in 1923, and reelection in 1928, serving until 1931. Following years of service as Honolulu

Postmaster, then Territorial Director of the Office of Social Security, he was drafted by the Democratic Party for its mayoral candidate in 1946, at age 74.

He was elected Mayor again in 1946 and reelected in 1948, 1950, and 1952. Such was the affection the people of O'ahu had for Johnny Wilson. He served as Mayor for more than 16 years and he was over eighty years old when his last term was completed. It is a rare *hapa-haole* (half-Caucasian) who did as much for O'ahu as did beloved Johnny Wilson.

❖   ❖   ❖

The tale is oft-told about how the forces of Kalanikupule were defeated by Kamehameha's army and driven over the Pali precipice to their deaths. Much is known of warrior-king Kamehameha I but there is little mention of the losers in this battle. Consider, for example, the story of High Chief Kaiana who dared to oppose Kamehameha.

HIGH CHIEF KAIANA

A decisive battle that ended over 200 years ago at the gateway to Windward O'ahu led to the creation of the Kingdom of Hawai'i. The story has never been told from the perspective of a warrior-chief on the losing side. When Kaiana (1756?-1795) was born, of chiefly parentage, each island was ruled by one or more chiefs. Disputes among them were settled by battle. To be a chief was to be possessed of extra strength and dexterity as a prerequisite to survival.

Kaiana was raised as a chief-to-be from birth on the island of Kaua'i. He learned how to fashion and hurl a spear, to sling stones, to trip and strangle an adversary, and the brute strength work of hand-to-hand combat. Kaiana grew to be a tall, athletic man and all a chief should be. He was inquisitive and shrewd. In this regard he was probably the equal of Kamehameha. It was to lead to his downfall.

In 1787 the island of Kaua'i was visited by an English merchant ship captained by John Meares. Captain Meares wanted to take a Hawaiian along with him to Canton in China, and chose the young chief Kaiana. The English captain described him thus: "Kaiana was about thirty-two years of age; he was near six feet five in stature, and the muscular form of his limbs was of a Herculean appearance. His carriage was replete with dignity, and having lived in the habit of receiving the respect due to superior rank in his own country, he possessed an air of distinction, which we will not suppose could suffer any diminution from his observation of European manners...."

Kaiana traded aggressively in Canton and accumulated a generous collection of silks, china ware, a supply of muskets and ammunition.

High Chief Kaiana. *(Lithograph by Joseph Woodcock; 1787)*

In 1788 he returned to Hawai'i on a merchant ship captained by the Englishman William Douglas. Before leaving Kaua'i, Kaiana and his brothers had angered their ruler (Kaeokulani; 1748-1794), and Kaiana was wary of events in his absence, so he asked Douglas to take him elsewhere in the islands. Captain Douglas stood off the Big Island of Hawai'i, learned that Kaiana was welcome, and Kaiana went ashore.

Kamehameha was chief of the island and he hungered for dominion over all the islands in order to unite them under himself as king. He saw in Kaiana a valuable and powerful ally, with his large collection of firearms and ammunition, so Kamehameha turned half of his army over to Kaiana in preparation for the battles yet to come.

Kaiana took his assignment to heart and worked at building the strength of his and Kamehameha's army. Kaiana's menacing attitude did not go unnoticed among *haole* visitors at this time. In 1792 the British naval captain George Vancouver (1758-1798) encountered Kaiana when he dropped anchor off the Big Island. Kaiana's attitude was so threatening to Vancouver that he mustered his men and put Kaiana ashore.

In late 1794 Kamehameha decided he had the strength to capture control of the northern-most islands. With Kaiana's help Kamahameha assembled a mighty expeditionary force of warriors and vessels, and was poised to move north from his base on Hawai'i. Cannons were mounted on sloops and muskets were issued. Wives and some children accompanied the warriors, Kaiana's wife among them. The expedition was launched in January 1795.

Maui fell to Kamehameha's armada with little resistance and Moloka'i was occupied next. The army paused and many councils were held there among the chiefs and *kahuna* (wise men).

It was here that Kaiana developed doubts as to his survival. More and more he found himself excluded from the councils of war. It seemed to him that he was in Kamehameha's disfavor and no man could survive Kamehameha's wrath. However, when the armada sailed for O'ahu, Kaiana was aboard his war canoe. He brooded over his prospects and during this passage he made a fatal decision.

When the fleet entered the channel, Kaiana jumped into his wife's canoe and rubbed noses with her. "Why this kiss?" she asked. He answered, "I am leaving you to follow the sons of my older brother (i.e. the defenders of O'ahu); but if I die, see that I am secretly buried." Kaiana's wife replied, "I will not follow you, for I must go with my chief; but if your side wins, find a secret place for my bones." After exchanging farewells the two parted. Kaiana deserted Kamehameha and he and his warriors made their way to join forces with the defenders of O'ahu.

Kaiana and his warriors landed at Kailua Beach. When he met Kalanikupule, the ruler-chief and defender of O'ahu, he lost no time in asserting himself. Kaiana was intimately acquainted with Kamehameha's forces and urged that a defense be organized with no time to lose. Kalanikupule's army decided to make their stand in Nu'uanu Valley leading to the Pali.

Kamehameha's armada landed on the beaches between Waikiki and Wai'alae. Skirmishing began near Punchbowl crater at the mouth of Nu'uanu Valley and a frontal assault began. Both sides had some cannons, warriors had a few muskets, and perhaps sixteen *haole* served Kamehameha as cannoneers and riflemen. The majority of the weapons on both sides were spears, stones, and daggers.

Midway up the valley was a small pond and substantial stone wall at a place called Pu'iwa (near today's Puiwa Road.) Kalanikupule's warriors took a position behind this wall. It was here that the pivotal battle was fought.

John Young (1749?-1835), Kamehameha's trusted expatriate Englishman aide, brought his cannon forward. The wall was breached with a cannon ball and Kamehameha's warriors pressed on. Kalanikupule's defenders began a retreat up the valley toward the Pali.

Accounts have it that the mighty warrior-chief Kaiana was wounded and captured at Pu'iwa. Russian naval officer Captain I. F. Lisianskii (1773-1837) brought his vessel to Hawai'i in 1804 where he encountered Kamehameha's trusted lieutenant John Young. Young told him he had been only a few paces away from Kaiana and witnessed his fall. The whole point of the spear that had pierced him protruded from his back. After the conflict, Young stated, Kaiana and many of his comrades were beheaded, and their heads stuck on the paling of a temple.

The end of the Nu'uanu Valley battle was dramatic as hundreds of warriors, women, and children were driven to their deaths over the Pali precipice. Kamehameha became the first king and ruler of the Kingdom of Hawai'i after High Chief Kaiana was slain.

CHAPTER FIVE

PALI LOOKOUT TO WAIKIKI

DURING A DRIVE down a picturesque remnant of the old Nuuanu Pali Road (now called Nuuanu Pali Drive), it is possible to imagine what it was like to live in Kailua and commute to Honolulu in those days before the present Pali Highway was completed. The stretch of road is beautiful, narrow, and winding, but could not accommodate today's heavy burden of trucks and buses.

NUUANU PALI DRIVE

Nuuanu Pali Drive winds through a bower of trees for almost three miles before rejoining the Nuuanu Pali Road. The winding and colorful road became obsolete when today's modern highway opened in 1957. A question arose about what to do about the old road. "Close it," said the practical-minded. "No, no," said the sentimental, "it's a beautiful stretch of tree-shaded road of which we have too few on O'ahu."

The sentimental-minded won out and this stretch of road remains as a bucolic bypass to the new road, rejoining the new

A typical stretch of Nuuanu Pali Drive. This narrow and winding road passes through a bower of trees for most of its length. This drive was once a portion of the only over-the-Pali road between Honolulu and Kailua. *(W. H. Dorrance)*

road north of Wood Street. A driver loses little time if he takes this bypass and, if he does, can recapture some of the mystique of old-time Oʻahu.

During this drive a pond and reservoir will be seen to the right. The reservoir played a key role in Honolulu's first street-light system, established in the last quarter of the nineteenth century. Water from the reservoir drove a hydroelectric generator that provided electricity for the system until it shut down in the early 1930s.

After rejoining the Nuuanu Pali Road you will enter a residential area starting at Wood Street that is the home of several prominent families.

NUUANU PALI ROAD

First-time visitors to Oʻahu can be forgiven if their thoughts center on Windward Oʻahu beaches and the Pali Lookout when they return to Waikiki via the Pali Highway. It's a different matter for residents. For them driving down the Pali Highway can be a lesson in Oʻahu's history when they think about the people and places behind the many roadside signs.

The Honolulu-bound Pali Highway becomes Nuuanu Pali Road upon exiting the tunnel under the lookout. Wood Street, four miles past the tunnel, is the first location of historical significance to be encountered. John H. Wood (1816-1892), Massachusetts born, first came to Oʻahu in 1846 on the brig *Henry* accompanied by other illustrious immigrants including Charles Reed Bishop (1822-1915), later husband of Princess Bernice Pauahi Bishop (1831-1884). Wood arrived with considerable financial strength and constructed the very first brick building in the city of Honolulu on Fort Street where he opened a shoe store.

Wood's initial stay on Oʻahu was short as, in 1849, he departed for California with his brother and others to add to his fortune by mining during the great gold rush. Apparently very successful, Wood returned to his native Massachusetts to marry Sarah Hardy and accumulate a large stock of merchandise. He then returned to Oʻahu in 1850 to stay, adding to his fortune by selling the goods.

Wood sent to Boston for a prefabricated house and erected it on a large tract of land near the present Wood Street. It was the family home for over thirty years. Here he raised sugarcane for a time until 1870 when he converted the property to a livestock ranch. The plantation was the first on the Honolulu side of the Ko'olau Mountain Range.

Perhaps it is not surprising that one of Wood's daughters, Florence Jones, became a long-time friend of Queen Emma. After all, they were practically neighbors when Queen Emma was at her Nuuanu Summer Palace. It was a close-knit society among the wealthy and *ali'i* (high chiefs) during the times of the Hawaiian monarchy, and much of it centered in the spacious homes located in Nu'uanu Valley.

Next is Dowsett Street. James Isaac Dowsett (1829-1898) is believed to be the first Caucasian child born in Hawai'i not of missionary parentage. Childhood friend of Kings Kamehameha IV, V, and Lunalilo, Dowsett made much of his opportunities by becoming a tycoon in island shipping and in ranching and sugarcane farming on Maui and O'ahu. He accumulated vast landholdings and later in life served in the House of Nobles during the reigns of King Kalakaua and Queen Lili'uokalani.

Dowsett and his wife, the former Annie Green Ragsdale, had thirteen children who were left with wide business and ranching interests, many surviving to this day. The Nu'uanu Valley location known as Dowsett Highlands is named for this *kama'aina* family.

The next sign of historical significance is for Puiwa Street. Over two-hundred years ago, in 1795, Kalanikupule decided to make a stand against the invading forces of Kamehameha I behind a stone wall located here. Kalanikupule's forces were defeated, and O'ahu was added to Kamehameha's domain.

One of the next signs indicates the location of Queen Emma's Summer Palace. Born Emma Kalanikaumakeamano, she was queen consort of Kamehameha IV whom she outlived by 19 years. Queen Emma was instrumental in founding the hospital that bears her name, as well as St. Andrews Episcopal Church and St. Andrews Priory School.

The Nuuanu Summer Palace is only one of several locations that served as Emma's summer residence. Allerton Gardens on Kaua'i in Lawai was once the location of one of the Queen's summer retreats. Another was located near the shore on the airport side of the entrance to Pearl Harbor. Later this location became Fort Kamehameha and is now integrated into the Hickam Air Force Base reservation. One wonders how Queen Emma was able to divide her attention among so many "summer palaces."

The last sign that catches the eye is attached to a substantial overpass denoting Wyllie Street. Robert Crichton Wyllie (1798-1865) was a Scotsman and bachelor businessman who arrived in Hawai'i 1844. His acumen attracted the notice of King Kamehameha III and, until his death in 1865, he served as minister of foreign affairs for Kings Kamehameha III and IV. He was an indefatigable letter writer, using that method to promote treaties to protect Hawai'i from the encroachment of foreign powers. His handwriting was almost indecipherable and one is puzzled as to how the recipients of his letters made perfect sense of them. Nevertheless, his efforts were successful as Hawai'i was able to stave off aggression by European powers during his stewardship. Wyllie founded Princeville Plantation on Kaua'i and was a stanch supporter of Queen Emma in her efforts to establish the Episcopal Church in Hawai'i.

Fort DeRussy! What a strange fort. No guns, no barracks, no fortifications of any kind to be seen. What can be seen is a well laid-out and well landscaped, park-like area open to all who wish to enjoy a tree-shaded stroll. How did this pleasant and peaceful place come to be called a fort?

It all began after the United States annexed the short-lived Republic of Hawaii in 1898. The annexation increased the number of U.S. assets requiring protection from bombardment by hostile naval powers of that day. Secretary of War William Howard Taft made an inspection trip to O'ahu in 1905 and subsequently recommended that fortifications be constructed to protect both Honolulu and Pearl Harbors. Congress appropriated the money and by 1915 two 6-inch caliber cannons were emplaced at Battery Dudley, and two 14-inch caliber cannons at adjacent Battery Randolph, both batteries located on the Army reservation that was named Fort DeRussy. The 6-inch guns could hurl a 108-pound, armor-piercing projectile 9 miles, and the 14-inch guns could hurl a 1,560 armor-piercing projectile 13.6 miles. Fort DeRussy was a very different place from the pleasant expanse that it is today when these large guns were active. The memories of persons who lived there during the latter years tell us what it was like.

LIVING AT OLD FORT DERUSSY

Today Fort DeRussy is a welcome greensward surrounded by the high rise buildings of Waikiki Beach. There is little there to suggest a fort and the newcomer can be pardoned for asking: "Why is this place called Fort DeRussy?" There is more than meets the eye. Long-time Lanikai resident Peggy Hickok Hodge relates the following:

Back in the early 1930s *kama'aina* Margaret "Peggy" Bairos was attending Roosevelt High School with classmate Monte Hickok, Jr. He was the son of Major Monte Hickok, commander of Fort DeRussy, and lived with his family in officers' quarters at the fort. When graduation time came, Major Hickok was pleased that his son and namesake had been awarded an appointment to the United States Military Academy at West Point. Young Monte's good friend and classmate, Peggy Bairos, enrolled at the University of Hawaii. It seemed they were destined to go separate ways.

But after a long-distance courtship conducted by letters during an eight-year separation, Peggy and Capt. Monte Hickok, Jr., Coast Artillery, got together in New York while he was stationed at Fort Totten. The long-distance romance was so unusual that Walter Winchell described it on one of his nationally-broadcast radio programs. During the reunion a pledge was made and they were married November 6, 1940 in a grand ceremony in Hampton, Virginia close by Fort Monroe, the citadel of the Coast Artillery Corps. It was an auspicious beginning.

In a wonderful coincidence, on April 1, 1941, Captain Hickok received orders transferring him to Fort DeRussy. It would be a return home for the young couple and they were delighted. They arrived, and were given quarters on "officer's row." Captain Hickok was assigned as battery officer of Battery D, 16th Coast Artillery Regiment in command of the soldiers serving the fort's anti-aircraft guns.

And what was life like at Fort DeRussy? "Wonderful," says Peggy, "our residence was a four-bedroom, three-bathroom house right on the beach. Monte and I went swimming every morning right off our beach." Every household chore was attended to by their live-in maid (a girl from one of the neighbor islands) or an enlisted man. Army life was quite different in those bygone days. There was a stiff regulation against "fraternizing" between officers and enlisted men. Yet enlisted men served the officers in many non-military ways.

Peggy found that she need not visit the commissary. All she had to do was leave the grocery list at a designated place on the lanai. An assigned enlisted man would pick it up, do the shopping at the commissary, and bring the groceries back to the officer's house. There he would store the groceries in the proper places in the pantry and refrigerator. This help, along with the maid, left Peggy much time to write, attend courses at the university, and to practice her music.

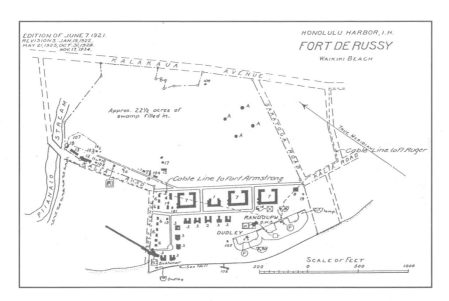

1930s War Department map of Fort Derussy. Arrow points to house occupied by the Hickoks and the dots denoted by "A" are the locations of the antiaircraft guns served by Captain Hickok's men. Note the proximity of the housing to Batteries Dudley and Randolph. *(National Archives)*

One day Peggy was playing the piano while an enlisted man attended to yard work nearby. The man was quite taken with Peggy's music and came to the window to compliment her. He asked that she play something by Debussy, which she did. It came out in their conversation that the soldier was a musician who had performed with the Chicago Symphony. Peggy told Monte about the encounter and they decided to entertain the enlisted man-musician at lunch. They did so next time he appeared to attend to the lawn.

As an example of what "fraternizing" meant in the old Army, Monte's commanding officer learned of the lunch with the enlisted man and Monte was sternly told "don't do that again."

The Hickok's Army quarters were very close to nearby Batteries Dudley and Randolph. When asked how often they fired those large caliber guns, Peggy replied, "Often, maybe once a month. And when they fired those guns it made the dishes jump off the shelves. They didn't always warn us in advance, either, like some have written."

The strict ban on fraternizing wasn't the only painful lesson about Army life that the young couple learned. A newly-assigned general admired the Hickok's beachside quarters. Captain Hickok was ordered to vacate and find quarters elsewhere so that the general and his family could take over. Peggy was six months pregnant at the time but that didn't matter. Fortunately, the Hickoks were able to find and rent a house in nearby Manoa Valley.

On November 28, 1941 the Army on O'ahu went on a "triple

Practice firing of one of Battery Randolph's 14-inch guns. Note the gun aimer perched next to the gun. The gun would be traversed until the gun aimer had the crosshairs of his telescope focused on a specific point on the target, and then the gun was fired. *(Postcard view; U.S. Army Museum of Hawai'i)*

alert." An attack was anticipated by the higher-ups, but the rank and file couldn't get excited about it. "Japan is so far away," was the prevailing opinion. Nevertheless, officers attended to their emergency missions. Captain Hickok's mission was to visit all the water and electric facilities in Honolulu and insure that they were intact and properly guarded. Monte didn't want to leave the very pregnant and bed-ridden Peggy alone so he carried her to his car and she made the inspection tour with him.

The Hickoks were at home that Sunday, December 7, 1941 morning when the Japanese attack came. Peggy's first child, a son, was born in February 1942 during the blackout in the tense months following the attack. Soon newly-promoted Major Hickok was assigned to Camp Davis in North Carolina and Peggy and son joined him at a nearby town. Her Fort DeRussy days were behind her. The spacious officer's quarters along with the rest of old Fort DeRussy's buildings were removed long ago to make way for the Hale Koa Hotel rest and recreation complex and today's pleasant vista. Only the excellent U.S. Army Museum of Hawaii, located within what used to be Battery Randolph, remains to remind the onlooker that Fort DeRussy was once a busy Coast Artillery Fort situated to protect Honolulu and its harbor from bombardment from offshore.

Major Hickok retired in 1944 and lived on as a teacher of Spanish language at Punahou School for seventeen years. Peggy, while being widowed, remarrying, and being widowed again, continued her prolific and remarkable career as a writer and author. She is pleased to point out that she has contributed newspaper columns for either the *Honolulu Advertiser* or the *Honolulu Star-Bulletin* over a span of 65 years. Two of her five books were released in 1996-1997. Peggy shows no signs of slowing up and continues to exercise, garden, play her beloved piano, and write.

Today it is impossible to repeat Peggy Hickok Hodge's experience of living at Fort DeRussy. The Coast Artillery was officially disbanded by the U.S. Army on June 28, 1950. The guns of Fort DeRussy, along with the cannon at other O'ahu forts, were cut up by scrappers. Fort DeRussy was designated as an Armed Forces Recreation Area in June 1949 and continues in that role.

Fort DeRussy's antiquated facilities served as the site for rest and recreation on through the Korean War. It wasn't until after the United States entered the Vietnam War that serious attention was directed to making a change. Finally, in 1969, a decision was made to use unappropriated funds to improve the facilities. The Corps of Engineers was awarded a contract for site preparation, beach restoration, and demolition of Batteries Randolph and Dudley. Next came the construction of the high-rise hotel Hale Koa (house of the warrior). The 15-story, 416-room military facility opened its doors in 1976 to all active and retired members of the uniformed services. The hotel was renovated and enlarged in 1993-1995 and enjoys year around occupancy.

Battery Dudley succumbed to the wreckers ball, but Battery Randolph was another matter. All attempts to reduce the massive reinforced concrete structure were futile. Finally, in 1976, the Army decided to house the U.S. Army Museum of Hawaii in the structure. The museum and visitor center describing the activities of the Corps of Engineers in the Pacific has proven to be a popular attraction for walk-in visitors who enjoy views of well- designed exhibits that depict the history of the U.S. Army in Hawai'i. No visit to Waikiki is complete without a visit to this fine museum.

WAIKIKI

Legends tell us that it was the great Chief Mailikukahi who, in the fifteenth century, first established Oahu's government at Waikiki. He is remembered for his wise and patient leadership, and setting the boundaries of Oahu's ancient *moku* and *ahupua'a*. Waikiki was the largest *ahupua'a* in the southern area and the seat of Oahu's government remained there until 1807 when Kamehameha I moved it closer to Honolulu's harbor.

Fort DeRussy is the first historic place encountered when entering Waikiki Beach from the west end. The fort's reservation occupies the lands known by the ancient Hawaiians as Kalia and when first occupied by the U.S. Army it was called "Military Reservation at Kalia, Waikiki, T.H.". The government purchased the 72-acre reservation in 1904 with the intention of emplacing two, two-gun batteries of coast defense guns on the site. This didn't sit well with local residents, many of whom owned nearby beach houses.

Sanford B. Dole (1844-1926), was appointed governor by President McKinley after service as the president of the short-lived republic and before that, as an associate justice of the kingdom's supreme court. Governor Dole made known his feelings to the Secretary of War: "...the firing of coast artillery guns in the vicinity of the residential district would not be desirable..." Notwithstanding, the government aquired the acreage and we have the now-disbanded War Department to thank for one of the last relatively open expanses on Waikiki Beach.

In 1909 the reservation was named "Fort De Russy" after deceased Bvt. Brig. Gen. Rene Edward De Russy (unk.-1865), who had served with distinction during the War of 1812 and for decades afterwards with the Corps of Engineers.

Governor Dole need not have feared frequent firing of the large guns emplaced at the fort. Records show that the largest, two

14-inch caliber monsters, were fired on average no more than twice a year in the thirty years of active use, and much of the practice firing occurred during World Wars I and II. By 1950 the guns were gone and the 14-inch gun battery structure, Battery Randolph, now houses the popular U. S. Army Museum of Hawaii and the Corps of Engineers Visitor Center.

Moving east (or "Diamond Head" as the vernacular has it) from Kalia, the locations where chiefs lived were called Kawehewehe, Helumoa, and Ulukou. Today these are occupied by the Halekulani, Royal Hawaiian, and Moana Hotels, respectively. Helumoa was known for its royal coconut grove, remnants of which survive within the Royal Hawaiian's east courtyard.

In 1925, Edward D. Tenney (1859-1934), president of the Matson company, presided over a grand scheme to increase the numbers of affluent visitors to then sparsely-visited Waikiki. A luxurious 650-passenger ocean liner, *Malolo,* was to be constructed by Matson to bring mainlanders to Oahu where they would be ensconced in the elegant Royal Hawaiian Hotel to be erected by Matson's partner in the venture, Territorial Hotel Company. A self-supporting golf and country club, later becoming Waialae Country Club, was to be built as an adjunct to the hotel.

The Royal Hawaiian Hotel opened February 1, 1927 and within a few months the fully-occupied *Malolo* embarked on its maiden voyage from San Francisco. A real Hawaiian reception awaited *Malolo's* arrival, including two dozen canoes manned by high-born Native Hawaiians bearing gifts, warriors, and hula girls, and a shore concert by the Royal Hawaiian Band. It was Oahu's grandest reception ever.

Improved and re-named *Matsonia* in 1937, the vessel served on until sold in 1948, keeping the hotel occupied. By then airplanes were increasing their share of the visitor market and the time of luxury liners was nearing an end. An era ended for the Matson Company when, on June 4, 1959 the Royal Hawaiian was sold to the Sheraton hotel chain. Nevertheless, the hotel lives on as one of Waikiki's most elegant and well-positioned hostelries.

However it was the Moana Hotel that originally established modern amenities on Waikiki Beach. Informally known as "The First Lady of Waikiki" and designed by prominent architect Oliver G. Traphagen, the Victorian and Beaux Arts Moana was inaugurated in March 1901 with a booking of over one hundred visiting Shriners. The new hotel was thoroughly modern and possessed a dedicated

The Moana Hotel showing the tramway that ran some three miles to downtown Honolulu. *(Hawaii State Archives)*

electrical plant, an elevator serving five levels, and seventy-five rooms and suites, each with a bathroom and telephone. Early advertisements stressed that one of the hotel's advantages was being located on the tramway line just three miles from downtown Honolulu. Two wings were added in 1918, and in March 1989 owner Kokusai Kogyo Company completed an extensive 21-month renovation of the hotel that included restoration of its original facade. The Moana is listed on the Hawaii State and National Registers of Historic Places.

Next to be encountered as you move Diamond Head along Kalakaua Avenue are the four "wizard stones." These are located next to the Waikiki police substation on the beach side of Kalakaua opposite the Hyatt Regency Hotel. The stones were carried, dragged, or hauled two miles from Kaimuki to the beach by Native Hawaiians sometime before 1400 A.D. in order to commemorate the visit of four wise men from Tahiti. Legend has it that before vanishing, Kapaemahu, Kahaloa, Kapuni, and Kinohi transferred their healing powers to these stones during a consecration ceremony.

A statue of one of Hawaii's most famous and beloved men, Duke Paoa Kahanamoku (1890-1968), backed by his long surfboard, has been placed a few steps Diamond Head of the wizard stones. A superb swimmer, Duke represented the United States in the 1912, 1920, 1928, and 1932 Olympic Games and won first-place medals in all but the last. He was elected sheriff of Honolulu in 1934, and when that office was abolished in 1961, he was appointed official city greeter and served as such until his death.

Duke possessed well-developed powers of observation. Kailua resident John Miholick (b. 1899) served in the Army at Fort DeRussy in the early 1920s. This was before the War Memorial Natatorium opened in 1927 and Duke swam every day off Fort DeRussy Beach. One day Duke offered to teach John how to swim. It was to no avail. The wiry Miholick just couldn't float. "John," said Duke, "there's something wrong with your lungs. You can't swim because you don't have enough air in your lungs!" It turned out Duke was correct. Miholick had been gassed in France during World War I, and this was the first time he was made to realize that his lung capacity had been seriously depleted. It was before the time of widespread use of chest X-rays and otherwise John had no way of learning the source of his problem.

Kuhio Beach is located one quarter mile Diamond Head of Duke's statue at a place the ancient Hawaiians knew as Kuekaunahi. Prince Jonah Kuhio Kalaniana'ole kept his residence there until the end of his life. Prince Kuhio was the grandson of Kaumuali'i (1780?-1824), last king of Kaua'i, and cousin of King Kalakaua. Childless King Kalakaua designated Prince Kuhio and his two older brothers as heirs to the throne after his sister Lili'uokalani. When Queen Lili'uokalani was deposed and the United States annexed the resulting short-lived republic in 1898, Prince Kuhio entered politics. In 1902 he was elected the territory's delegate to Congress, an office he filled until his death. The last heir to the throne passed when Prince Kuhio died and his was the last state funeral held for an *ali'i*. He was buried at the Royal Mausoleum in Nu'uanu Valley. His residence and lands were given to the city to become Kuhio Beach Park, and a small plaque affixed to the seawall in commemoration. The more-recently constructed Honolulu federal building bears his name.

The Honolulu Aquarium is located a little over one-half mile Diamond Head of Kuhio Beach just before the War Memorial Natatorium. The present structure is the third aquarium built on the site and the location has a history of its own. In 1900 the Honolulu Rapid Transit & Land Company (H.R.T.& L.), a street railway system, had been chartered but was seriously under-capitalized. James B.

Castle, his brother, and his father's estate stepped in and purchased controlling stock in order to supply the shortfall in funds. By 1904 the H.R.T.& L. was running street cars down King Street and on to Waikiki's Kalakaua Avenue, replacing the mule-powered tramway that had served Waikiki Beach since about 1890. However, the new streetcar system needed a boost in traffic so members of the Castle and Cooke families came to the rescue.

Mrs. James B. Castle and Mrs. Charles M. Cooke (1853-1934) donated land and the H.R.T.& L. built the first aquarium. It opened in 1904 and was an immediate success. Partly because of this, the King Street to Waikiki route became the most profitable H.R.T.& L. streetcar line. For the next thirty-two years the streetcar line prospered until it was replaced with trolley buses in 1938.

This completes your East O'ahu tour

PART TWO

CENTRAL O'AHU TOUR

Driving time: Three hours plus time for side trips and stops for lunch and the beaches.

TheBus time: Four hours plus time for stops.

INTRODUCTION TO CENTRAL O'AHU

THIS TOUR IS the most popular of the three described in the book because you see a larger expanse of the island than the other two tours. However, all three have much of historical interest and it would be difficult to select one over the others when it comes to cultural significance.

For convenience, it is assumed that you begin your tour in Waikiki Beach. Of course you can join the tour anywhere along the way.

From Waikiki you should drive inland and turn left on Ala Wai Boulevard. Keep in the right-hand lane and turn right and over the bridge at McCully Street. Drive 3/4 mile along McCully Street, over a highway bridge, to the intersection with Dole Street. Turn left onto Dole and drive a short three blocks to Alexander Street where you turn left toward the Highway H-1 access ramp. Enter the highway (Lunalilo Freeway) heading west. Signs on McCully, Dole, and Alexander Streets point directions to the Highway H-1.

Drive a little over 3-1/2 miles along Highway H-1 until you reach the intersection with Likelike Highway passing the access road to the Nuuanu Pali Road along the way. Passing up the Nuuanu Pali Road to Windward O'ahu is intentional. The East O'ahu tour returned you to Waikiki via the Nuuanu Pali Road and there is no need to repeat the experience. Turn right onto Likelike Highway and you are on your way to Windward O'ahu. Taking the Likelike Highway to Windward O'ahu exposes you to a different part of the island.

As an alternative to driving Likelike Highway, you can include the trans-Ko'olau Interstate Highway H-3 in your central O'ahu tour. To do so after entering west-bound Highway H-1, you must continue west past the Likelike Highway turn-off and onto the Moanalua Freeway, state highway 78. The Highway H-3 entrance road appears after two miles and taking it starts the trans-Ko'olau journey. About ten miles after entering the highway, and after leaving the second of the highway tunnels on the windward side of the Ko'olau range, you must take the egress marked "To Kaneohe" in order to circle back to join the Likelike Highway. Once on the Likelike Highway you proceed on the tour and little is lost while a view of undeveloped Halawa Valley is gained.

It is left to you to choose the highway for crossing the Ko'olau Range. Little is lost with either choice and the remaining eighty-five percent of the tour is identical once the Likelike Highway is rejoined on the Windward side.

When you reach the busy intersection of the Likelike Highway with Kamehameha Highway, route 83, turn left here to enter the community of Kane'ohe. Drive Kamehameha Highway, route 83, for the next 40 miles until you pass through the North Shore community of Hale'iwa. There are several interesting communities along the way.

A side trip is needed to visit Kawailoa, one of the last sugar plantation camps surviving on O'ahu. Located about one mile *mauka* of Highway 83 some ten miles beyond Turtle Bay, a visit to Kawailoa does much to reveal plantation living as it used to be. Hale'iwa is the next North Shore town encountered along Highway 83 three miles beyond Kawailoa. To appreciate the town you should take the right-hand fork into the center of town, and not the Kamehameha Highway by-pass road when approaching Hale'iwa.

Hale'iwa marks the westernmost point of your Central O'ahu Tour. As you exit Hale'iwa the tour turns toward Waikiki via a trip through the center of the island. However, drivers have the flexibility to make a side trip into the plantation town of Waialua where both the sugarmill and the town can be examined with little loss in time. To make this side trip, you exit Hale'iwa and encounter a traffic circle, "Weed Circle." Take the right-hand Waialua Beach Road branch and continue two miles to Puuiki Road. Turn left at Puuiki Road and proceed 3/4 mile to the sugarmill, easily in view all the way. Turn right at the mill and examine it as you drive by to enter "mill camp."

Resume the tour by retracing your path to Kealahanui Road facing the sugarmill. Turn right at Goodale Avenue and drive a little over 1/2 mile through Waialua town to turn left onto Farrington Highway, Highway 930. At the next corner the highway becomes Kaukonahua Road, Highway 803. Continue on Kaukonahua southbound and you are on your way to Wahiawa.

Wahiawa is six miles south of the Waialua entrance to Kaukonahua Road, Highway 803. Taking the left fork about 4 miles after entering Highway 803, Kaukonahua Road, results in very shortly joining Kamehameha Highway, Highway 80, bypassing the Schofield reservation, passing through Waihiawa town, and entering Honolulu-bound Highway H-2. About 3/4 mile after entering Highway 80, and shortly before the Whitmore Avenue intersection, you will encounter the location of the ancient Birth Stones of Kukaniloko on the right. A short drive leads to the parking area close to the stones.

If you skip the Birth Stones visit, take the right fork at Highway 803 to enter Wilikina Drive just before Wahiawa that results in passing Schofield Barracks on the right. Those desiring to visit the military museum on the Barracks reservation should turn right into the reservation at the Macomb gate. Schofield Barracks is an "open base" and civilians are free to enter as of this writing (1998). A short drive down Macomb Road takes you to the intersection with Waianae Avenue. The Tropic Lightning Museum is directly in front of the intersection and you can park to the right of the museum building after circling the block to enter the parking lot from the correct direction. You know you have found the museum when you see the armored personnel carrier, Sherman tank, and two artillery pieces parked on the lawn.

Retracing the drive into the Schofield reservation, you turn right onto Highway 803, which quickly becomes Highway 99 leaving Wahiawa. You have seen little of the town because the highway skirts the edge of the community.

Almost 1-1/2 miles after you turn right onto Highway 99 from Macomb Road, you enter Highway H-2 southbound for

Honolulu. The next 9-1/2 miles take you toward the junction with Highway H-1 on a gently downward slope, now sparsely developed but as recently as 1980 devoted to sugarcane farming on both sides of the highway. The lochs of Pearl Harbor are plainly visible toward the end of this stretch, as is the island in the harbor known as Ford Island. Turn left onto the Honolulu-bound lane of Highway H-1, Lunalilo Freeway, when you reach the intersection. Some 4-1/2 miles down the highway you reach a fork in the freeway. Continue on the Highway H-1 fork that takes you past the airport on the elevated freeway.

Take the Nimitz Highway off-ramp at the end of the elevated H-1 freeway. Shortly after you enter Nimitz you will pass Sand Island access road. Remember where it is. You may want to return during your visit in order to drive to the end of the road on the island where there is a State Recreation Area from which you can enjoy an excellent view of the piers, wharves, and high-rise buildings of Honolulu across the busy harbor.

As you pass the Aloha Tower Marketplace on the right, take note of the Hawaii Maritime Center, an excellent repository of Hawai'i's rich maritime history. The tall masts of the *Falls of Clyde* sailing ship stand out as she is tied up next to the museum. Just beyond the museum is ample public parking, and a return to visit the museum is strongly recommended.

Sailing ship *Falls of Clyde* tied up at pier 7 next to the Hawaii Maritime Center. Launched in Scotland in 1878, this sailing ship served the Matson Navigation Company from 1898 to 1906. *(W. H. Dorrance)*

Nimitz Highway becomes Ala Moana Boulevard after you pass the museum and you are now but 2-1/2 miles from the entrance to Kalakaua Avenue and your starting point. Including side trips, you have driven about 88 miles and are now as well-informed about much of O'ahu's history as is many a *kama'aina*.

DIRECTIONS FOR TAKING THEBUS

Starting in Waikiki, walk to Kuhio Avenue and board Ala Moana-bound bus nos. 8, 19, 20, or 58, and ask the driver for a transfer. Transfer at Ala Moana to bus no. 55 for the round-the-island tour. Bus no. 55 becomes bus no. 52 at Turtle Bay and returns you to Ala Moana where you must transfer to bus nos. 8, 19, 20 or 58 to return to your starting point.

TheBus takes the Nuuanu Pali Highway rather than the Likelike Highway and will not make side trips for visiting the North Shore communities of Waialua and Kawailoa, the Birth Stones, and Schofield Barracks. Be sure to take a supply of dollar bills for reboarding a bus after every stop you plan to make along the way. Bus drivers do not make change. Routes and times sometimes change so call 848-5555 to confirm your plans.

CHAPTER SIX

WAIKIKI BEACH TO KANE'OHE

IF YOU STARTED your tour in Waikiki you were exposed to a bit of Hawai'i's history when you traversed McCully, Dole, and Alexander Streets on your way to Highway H-1. These are all prominent family names in Hawai'i. Lawrence McCully was a Supreme Court justice during King Kalakaua's rule; Sanford Ballard Dole served as a Supreme Court justice under the monarchy, president of the short-lived Provisional Government of the Republic of Hawaii, and, following annexation, as the Territory of Hawaii's first governor; William Patterson Alexander (1805-1884) arrived in Hawai'i in May 1832 with the fifth company of American missionaries. His son, Samuel Thomas Alexander (1836-1904) founded the Alexander & Baldwin conglomerate with his brother-in-law Henry Perrine Baldwin (1842-1911).

Then there is the Lunalilo Freeway, Highway H-1. William Charles Lunalilo, grandson of a half-brother of Kamehameha I, has the distinction of being the first Hawaiian monarch who ascended to the throne via a constitutionally-mandated election, held in 1873 because King Kamehameha V (1830-1872) died without naming a successor. Lunalilo reigned for little over a year then died of tuberculosis. His will called for establishing the Lunalilo Home for infirm and destitute people of Hawaiian blood which serves that purpose to this day. Lunalilo was succeeded by David Kalakaua in the election of 1874.

The right-hand corner of the turn from Lunalilo Freeway onto the Likelike Highway is the location of Bishop Museum, by far the most significant repository of Polynesian artifacts in existence. The museum was established in trust by Charles Reed Bishop in memory of his wife, Bernice Pauahi Bishop, who preceded him in death. This museum deserves hours of thoughtful inspection but it is not intended to be visited on this tour. However, those interrupting the tour to visit the museum can turn right at Bernice Street, the first intersection after turning onto Likelike Highway, and follow the directions on roadside signs.

Likelike Highway was named for Miriam Kapili Likelike (1851-1887), sister of future monarchs David Kalakaua and Lydia Lili'uokalani, wife of Archibald S. Cleghorn (1835-1910), and mother of heir to the throne Princess Victoria Ka'iulani (1875-1899). Young Princess Ka'iulani died in sorrow after the overthrow of the monarchy in 1893 and the annexation by the United States in 1898. Her death removed the ranking *ali'i*-claimant to the throne, much to the despair of those who sought the restoration of the Hawaiian monarchy.

The journey up the valley on Likelike Highway to the Wilson tunnel (named for Old Pali Highway constructor and longtime Honolulu mayor Johnny Wilson) is unexceptional except for the wooded watershed in the upper reaches of Kalihi Valley. However, the panoramic views from the Likelike Highway after exiting the tunnel are dazzling. Mokapu Peninsula is off in the right center. The hangars and concrete apron of Kaneohe Marine Corps Station Hawai'i stand out on the site of a royal preserve of the ancient Hawaiian *ali'i*.

This locality wasn't always a Marine Corps base. The story of its existence is an important part of O'ahu's history.

Enhanced view of former NAS-Kaneohe as seen from exit of Likelike Highway tunnel. These hangars once housed Navy flying boats and were built in 1939-1940. Note the concrete aprons at the water's edge which were used to haul the flying boats onto the shore. *(W. H. Dorrance)*

An Infamous Day on Windward O'ahu

A major naval air station once existed on Windward O'ahu for only six years.

In 1938 the United States was increasingly concerned about the aggressive Japanese expansion into the Pacific. Japan was restricting access to the Pacific island trust territories ceded to it at the end of World War I, while waging war with China and building up a modern navy far beyond treaty limits. There was ample reason for the United States to be suspicious of Japanese intentions and its Pacific flank was exposed. It was time to take precautionary measures.

Congress directed the Secretary of the Navy to assess United States readiness in the Pacific area. He assigned the task to a committee led by retired Admiral Hepburn. Late in 1938 the committee made

Consolidated PBY flying boat of the type stationed at NAS-Kaneohe. "The eyes and ears of the fleet." These aircraft were manufactured by the Consolidated Aircraft Co. located in San Diego, California. *(W. H. Dorrance collection)*

its recommendations: a vast network of Naval air bases should be constructed on the U. S. territorial islands of O'ahu, Wake, Midway, Johnston, Palmyra and Guam. No time should be lost. The new long-range Consolidated Catalina Navy PBY flying boats required suitable forward bases.

Congress acted promptly. In early 1939 the Navy was authorized to begin the large Pacific Naval Air Base (PNAB) construction project. There have been few projects as wide in scope or as geographically dispersed as was PNAB. Assembling qualified contractors was a major effort and time was of the essence.

The pearl of the effort was the construction of the Naval Air Station (NAS) on Mokapu Peninsula. The project began in 1939 and was almost completed by December 1941. Millions of cubic yards of earth and coral were dredged from Kane'ohe Bay and used as fill to create an air field on the peninsula. The dredging also created a landing and takeoff run for seaplanes.

The station began operations even before construction was completed. By the end of 1940, thirty-six twin-engine PBY seaplanes were assigned to the NAS and patrolling the Pacific. During times of tension, these aircraft rotated on round-the-clock patrols in the surrounding Pacific and were regarded as "the eyes and ears of the fleet."

However, in 1941 the base commander had little besides a few rifles and machine guns to defend the base in the unlikely event of an attack, and it was standard practice that such weapons and ammunition were stored under lock and key. On the morning of December 7, 1941, three PBYs were on patrol. The remaining thirty-three airplanes were either in Kaneʻohe Bay at mooring, on the ramp, or in the hangars. It was a quiet Sunday morning.

At 7:48 a.m. several Japanese Zero fighter planes swept down on Kaneohe Naval Air Station, and for the next 15 minutes they wheeled back and forth at low altitude, strafing every object in sight. Nothing was spared. All of the grounded aircraft, vehicles, hangars and even barracks and residences drew fire. Several survivors reported that some Japanese pilots smiled with confidence and waved as they flew by at slow speeds and low altitudes.

Destruction on the NAS-Kaneohe ramp following the December 7, 1941 Japanese attack. Thirty-three out of thirty-six of the flying boats were disabled or destroyed during the attack. (U.S. Navy)

Defenders were few and disorganized. They had to shoot the locks off storage magazines to get at the supply of guns and ammunition.

Twenty-five minutes later a second wave of Japanese fighters and bombers swept in to finish the job. The attack could not have been more effective. All thirty-three PBYs on the ground were rendered inoperative or damaged beyond repair. The hangars and ground support facilities were heavily damaged. There were seventeen American dead and sixty-seven wounded, including civilians.

The attacking Japanese lost only one pilot, flight leader Japanese Navy Lieutenant Iida. Accounts are mixed but at least one by a surviving pilot in Iida's flight suggests that Iida died in a suicide plunge. He had signalled that his damaged plane would not make it back to his launching carrier.

The first attack on NAS Kaneohe occurred some seven minutes before the fleet at anchor was attacked at Pearl Harbor. When the strike at Kaneohe began, at least two telephone calls to other military bases were made to alert them. It was all in vain. The surprise was complete and the consequences devastating, as has gone down in history.

After World War II, the Navy no longer needed NAS Kaneohe. The station was deactivated in 1946 and put into mothballs. In 1952 the Marine Corps took possession and reopened the base as Marine Corps Air Station-Kaneohe (today Marine Corps Base Hawaii), home of the 1st Marine Amphibious Brigade.

Only a few aged veterans remember the details of that terrible day that occurred over fifty years before this was written.

About mid-way down the Likelike Highway toward Kane'ohe, the driver encounters a rich stand of banana trees on both sides of the highway. Few are aware that bananas are a cash crop for Hawai'i and this plantation is one of Hawai'i's largest. It seems that the cool shading of the nearby Ko'olau *pali* creates a day-around temperature that is perfect for growing bananas. Those taking TheBus will encounter a smaller and abandoned banana plantation on the right side of Kailua Road just after passing Maunawili Valley and Mount Olomana.

When you look over and beyond the banana plantation from Likelike Highway, you see the twin concrete roadways of Highway H-3 in the distance. Construction of this engineering marvel took thirty years to complete.

Highway H-3

The origins of Federal Highway H-3 have been obscured by decades of acrimony and dispute involving archaeological, aesthetic, safety, cultural, environmental and other concerns. It is sometimes forgotten that this project had its beginnings when the country was at war in Vietnam. At that time Federal Highway H-3 was justified because it strengthened the nation's defense. This was consistent with the principles enunciated by President Eisenhower when he launched the interstate highway program. The thinking was that military traffic would move more smoothly and rapidly between the Marine Station (now Base) on Mokapu Peninsula, and the Naval reservation at Pearl Harbor when Highway H-3 was completed.

The project moved forward by fits and starts starting with preliminary planning by the State in 1959. Opened to the public in December 1997, the 15-mile long highway cost the taxpayers a record-breaking one-hundred million dollars per mile. Even then, it wasn't easy to get this far.

Responding to the cries of preservationists and environmentalists, the Honolulu side of the trans-Ko'olau highway was moved from Moanalua Valley to Halawa Valley. Next, the Kane'ohe side right-of-way was displaced to avoid violating the location of Kukui-o-Kane *heiau*. (It had already been grossly violated in the early 1920s by now-gone pineapple plantings by Libby, McNeil & Libby Pineapple Company. Failure of that company's efforts in the early 1920s has been attributed by Hawaiians to the destruction of this large *heiau*. It wouldn't do to jeopardize the success of the Highway H-3 by repeating Libby, McNeil's mistake.) Then, the course of the highway through Halawa Valley was moved to accommodate a newly-discovered ancient Hawaiian archaeological site. All of these moves served to delay schedules and increase costs, of course.

Drivers were treated to some of the most spectacular vistas in the islands when the highway was completed. Starting at the Halawa end near Aloha Stadium, you drive over and through the greenery of Halawa Valley, though a trans-Ko'olau tunnel, and out onto a ridge-hugging viaduct in Ha'iku Valley. Here you will enjoy a view over the valley and out beyond Kane'ohe Bay and Mokapu Peninsula.

After passing through another tunnel, you snake through banana trees and around Hoomaluhia Park to finish the final hilly and rustic run to the gates of Marine Corps Base Hawaii on Mokapu Peninsula.

The cost of the project mirrored the contracting team assembled to complete it. The principal players were the State of Hawai'i, Department of Transportation, and the overall design contractor. As of December, 1992, the design contractor managed seven design consultants, who, in turn, managed thirty-two sub-consultants. DOT for its part managed nineteen prime construction contracts. These numbers suggest the complexity of the project.

Every effort was made to minimize costs despite the complexity. It was decided to cast the viaduct's concrete segments at one central location at the Kane'ohe end. This decision was estimated to save some $2.2 million and four to six months of construction time. A special iron oxide pigment was added to the concrete aggregate in order that it match the color of indigenous rock outcropping. The segments are cemented in place with an epoxy glue.

The highway includes two tunnel systems. Twin tunnels have been excavated through the southern ridge bordering Ha'iku Valley and through the Ko'olau Mountains at the head of Ha'iku Valley. These tunnels are roughly half-circle in cross section with a width of 45 feet and height of 33 feet. An exploratory tunnel was dug beneath the intended path of the trans-Ko'olau tunnel to determine that the tunnels were above the water table.

Some of the more unusual aspects of constructing this highway were the precautions taken because of the proximity of the Omega Station in Ha'iku Valley. This station, run by the U. S. Coast Guard and now closed down, was one of eight worldwide and generated high voltage very low frequency (VLF) signals that were used in ocean navigation. Transmitter cables (removed in 1997) were suspended high above Ha'iku Valley and the H-3 viaduct passed beneath them. Construction workers were protected from the effects of any exposure to the VLF electromagnetic field by wearing rubber boots and rubber safety gloves when handling reinforcement steel or working with cranes in damp weather. Vehicles were grounded and no gasoline engines were refueled in the vicinity.

During times of peace most of us are not unduly concerned with the advantages of Highway H-3 for the military. We tend to think about peacetime advantages and, for Highway H-3, they are there: the new residential area at Kapolei, Campbell Industrial Park, and the burgeoning "second city" developments on the 'Ewa plain. One prominent politician projected that when Highway H-3 opened "one third of Windward O'ahu commuters will use the Pali Highway, one third the Likelike Highway, and the remaining third will travel in the 'Ewa direction using H-3." Highway H-3 promises to stimulate growth and prosperity throughout O'ahu.

Once a scattered collection of a few frontier, mom-and-pop general stores with perhaps 1,000 residents, Kane'ohe now boasts a population of some 37,000 people. Today the town presents a haphazard, strip-mall appearance. But Kane'ohe has a rich history of its own.

OLD KANE'OHE TOWN

Today Kane'ohe town fills much of the *ahupua'a* of Kane'ohe and He'eia. Kane'ohe means "bamboo man," one who is cruel (cutting), and legend has it that such a man lived in Kane'ohe. "He'eia" was the name of the grandson of the demigod Olopana. In less than 150 years Kane'ohe and He'eia have made the transition from a scattering of *taro* patches and fishponds to that of a thriving community. The combined population of He'eia and Kane'ohe was about 2,000 when Capt. James Cook discovered the Hawaiian Islands for Europeans in 1778. Archeological evidence indicates that those 2,000 people enjoyed a healthy existence.

Kane'ohe was one of the most terraced regions in the islands. Terraces bulwarked with stone ramparts contained planting of *taro,* potatoes, breadfruit, and bananas. He'eia, Kea'ahala, Kane'ohe, and Kawa streams, fed by upland streamlets and freshets, provided a source of water for irrigation. Four fishponds were constructed at the shore of He'eia and fourteen more along Kane'ohe's shoreline. Both *ahupua'a* were presided over by chiefs who parcelled out the land to commoners, shared the bounties of the fishponds, and maintained order.

The Hawaiians erected fifteen *heiau* throughout the two *ahupua'a* for religious observances. Bishop Museum archeologist Dr. J. Gilbert McAllister reported by 1933 four of these *heiau* had been destroyed. A study of a current map reveals that only five of the remainder have survived since then.

Some of the most interesting lands are on Mokapu Peninsula now occupied by the Marine Corps Base Hawaii. The peninsula's name is a contraction of the Hawaiian words *moku kapu* (sacred or forbidden place). The northern part of Mokapu is in He'eia *ahupua'a* and the southernmost portion is in Kane'ohe *ahupua'a*. A village, a *heiau,* fishing shrines, and burial sites were located in the northern portion of the peninsula toward Kane'ohe Bay.

In early times Mokapu was a resort forbidden to commoners where chiefs of both sexes and their retinues would enjoy games, feasting, and pageants. Mokapu's fishponds, Kaluapuhi, Nu'upia, and Halekou, were stocked with delectable fish intended for chiefly visitors. By Captain Cook's time the chiefs had moved to Waikiki and Mokapu was left to commoners.

Legends have it that the beach along the northern shore of Mokapu is the site of the origin of man. It was here that the god Kane first drew the outlines of man in the sand. "Live," and "Come to life," commanded the gods Ko, Lono, and Kane, and the first man sprang forth from the sands.

The sand dunes along this beach are a sacred Hawaiian burial site. During construction of the air base and, later, the golf course, over 500 burials were unearthed. Most of the bones were reburied in the dunes and the rest were examined by Bishop Museum's experts. They found that the average age at death was 35 years for males and 33 years for females.

Inroads by *haole* into Kane'ohe started with a land-use award made in 1821 by King Kamehameha II (Liholiho, 1796-1824) to the Spaniard Don Francisco de Paula Marin (Manini, 1774-1837), loyal servant and advisor to Kings Kamehameha I, II, and III. Then, following a short-lived attempt to set up a mission in the Marquesas Islands, in 1834 Congregational missionary minister Benjamin Wyman Parker (1803-1877) was stationed with his family in Kane'ohe. His memory has been perpetuated by naming Kane'ohe's Benjamin Parker Elementary School for him.

During the Great Mahele, King Kamehameha III divided the kingdom's lands into parcels owned by the government, the monarch, and the high chiefs. By 1850 commoners could petition for land ownership, too. However, the largest portions in He'eia and Kane'ohe were awarded to a chiefess and a high chief. Queen

Hakaleleponi (Harriet) Kapakuhaili Kalama (1817-1870), King Kamehameha III's consort, was awarded title to 9,500 acres of Kane'ohe *ahupua'a*. High Chief Abner Paki (1808-1855), father of Bernice Pauahi Bishop, received title to 3,737 acres, including the He'eia portion of Mokapu Peninsula. As for commoners, 208 awards were made in Kane'ohe and He'eia that were all less than ten acres in size. The awards opened the way for sale of the land to those bent on plantation development.

In 1865 Queen Kalama, in partnership with the Kingdom's minister of finance and foreign affairs, Charles Coffin Harris (1822-1881), planted sugarcane on her Kane'ohe land and erected a mill. After the queen's death in 1870 Harris purchased the land from her heir. Kaneohe Sugar Company went out of business in 1885 and the lands were incorporated as Kaneohe Ranch, after which they were purchased in 1907 by James B. Castle from Harris' daughter and heir. This was the beginning of Castle interests in Kane'ohe.

The Reciprocity Treaty of 1876 allowed duty-free importation of Hawaiian sugar into the United States, an advantage not granted to competing growers in Asia and the Caribbean. Those holding land in Kane'ohe and He'eia moved quickly to exploit the opportunity.

The Rev. Benjamin Parker purchased title to some fifty-five acres in Kane'ohe in 1855. By 1880 his son, the Rev. Henry Hodges Parker (1834-1927), had added ninety-five acres by lease and purchase, employed twenty workers, planted sugarcane, and was having it ground by the Kaneohe Sugar Company mill. He served as pastor of Honolulu's Kawaiahao Church for over fifty years in addition to growing sugarcane and ranching in Kane'ohe.

In 1891, during the short reign of Queen Lydia Lili'uokalani, firebrand Hawaiian legislator Robert W. Wilcox (1855-1903) proposed awarding Kane'ohe Bay to Great Britain as a coaling station. The Admiralty considered and rejected the idea as being unnecessary to British naval strategy. It was left to the U. S. Navy to establish a twentieth-century naval station in Kane'ohe Bay.

The next crop to thrive in Kane'ohe after the sugarcane was rice. Chinese farmers converted terraces and *taro* patches to rice paddies that soon filled the area occupied by today's subdivisions of Crown Terrace and Waikalua.

The population of He'eia and Kane'ohe remained stable at about 1,000 residents from 1853 to after 1900, and there was little in Kane'ohe that could be called a town. Except for the two large parcels that made up Heeia Agricultural Company and Kaneohe Ranch, the two *ahupua'a* consisted of a number of small farms.

Kane'ohe began to change after the turn of the century when the Pali Saloon opened on Kamehameha Highway opposite the He'eia sugarmill. The saloon was frequented by the plantation workers and served as a popular watering hole for transients bound for Honolulu or the North Shore. The saloon lingered on for several years after the plantation shut down in 1903.

An unusual enterprise came to Kane'ohe in 1912 when a trans-Pacific radio telegraph station was constructed at the shore in He'eia. For years the antenna towers were the tallest structures on O'ahu. The U. S. Navy took the facility over during World War I and eventually added two more antenna towers. The facility was shut down and removed shortly after the end of World War II. The large pyramidal concrete anchors for the cables that supported the towers can still be seen in Kane'ohe Bay.

1912 was a busy year for Kane'ohe. That year Libby, McNeil & Libby began leasing the lands of Heeia Agricultural Company, Kaneohe Ranch, and numerous other small parcels in He'eia, Kane'ohe, and Kailua for cultivating pineapple. The *taro* patches and rice paddies were soon planted in pineapple. Photographs taken from the Pali Lookout show a vast sea of pineapple fields where today's Kane'ohe lies.

Pineapple cultivation proved to be less profitable in Windward O'ahu than in central O'ahu. The small cannery at Kahalu'u was inadequate, the independent growers were inefficient, the land yielded less than was desired, a blight threatened crops, and growing costs were too high. By 1923 the end was near for pineapple in Windward O'ahu when the cannery shut down.

Rice and pineapple cultivation brought a steady influx of Japanese workers, many of whom desired to preserve the language and customs of the old country for their children. In 1908 a Japanese language school was started in He'eia. In 1922, another was opened in the Luluku section of Kane'ohe.

From 1920 to 1930 long-time territorial and city government official Lyman H. Bigelow (1878-1966) built a substantial estate with spacious gardens at the shore and called it "Dreamwood." After the Bigelows' deaths the residence was occupied by the non-profit Habilitat treatment center.

Mr. Bigelow was Kaneʻohe's most distinguished resident. Before his retirement, he served as Territorial Superintendent of Public Works. He directed the construction of wharves in Honolulu Harbor and Kewalo Basin, Hanalei Harbor on Kauaʻi, docks and port facilities at Hilo, and harbor improvements on Maui and Molokaʻi. His department supervised the construction of the Ala Wai Canal in Waikiki, the rehabilitation of Washington Place (governor's residence in Honolulu), and the Volcano House on the Big Island.

In July 1933 the Navy moved its radio intercept station from Wailupe to the Heʻeia location and surrounded it with a secure fence. Curiously, this important facility went untouched during the December 7, 1941 attack, then was dismantled in 1946.

As late as 1935 a water buffalo could be seen working in a rice paddy located *mauka* on Kamehameha Highway where the Kaneʻohe post office is located. By the late 1930s the stretch along Kamehameha Highway was beginning to fill with a scattering of shops and service stations. Eighteen fishponds marked the shoreline from Mokapu Peninsula to Heʻeia. The shore of Mokapu Peninsula facing Kaneʻohe Bay was occupied by beach houses and the rest of the peninsula was devoted to ranching and small farms.

Such was the rural settlement of Kaneʻohe in the days leading up to World War II.

Haiku Road marks the dividing line between the districts of Kaneʻohe and Heʻeia. When the Coast Guard's Omega station was operational you could reach the transmitter building by turning left here from Kamehameha Highway and driving deep into the valley on Haiku Road and a rugged extension. However, the station shut down in 1996 and much of what was one of the most exotic constructions undertaken during World War II has been dismantled. Nevertheless, its story is a part of Oʻahu's history, too.

HA'IKU VALLEY LADDER

Back in 1942, during World War II, the U. S. Navy needed a method to transmit messages over extra long distances. Long wavelength, very low frequency radio transmission was the answer. Such transmission takes advantage of the reflection of long wavelength radiation by the Earth's ionosphere.

Unfortunately, such transmission also required large antenna lengths, on the order of a mile long strung some 2,000 feet above the ground. Such a transmitting antenna had been strung between two small mountain peaks in Java, and the concept was known to work. The Navy looked for a suitable site in Hawai'i.

Ha'iku Valley, adjacent to the settlement of Kane'ohe, is one of a series of deep valleys formed by ridges of the Ko'olau mountain range on O'ahu. Brush and *kiawe* trees filled the valley in 1942 and the ridges tower some 3,200 feet over the valley floor. It was an ideal VLF antenna location. In 1943 the Navy's contractors began construction there.

Building the ground-based facilities like the transmitter building posed no special problems. It was stringing some 6,000 feet of heavy copper cable between the 3,200 foot high ridges that would present difficulties. Each length of antenna cable weighed several tons.

Hoisting the cable was done in stages. First a wooden ladder up the south Pali ridge (Pu'u Keahiakahoe) was assembled. This required slow and painstaking mountain climbing by experts who would advance ten feet then haul up and fasten another length of ladder. No helicopters were available in 1942.

The next stage involved carrying up steel and concrete for a hoist and housing. The hoist then hauled up materials for heavy antenna anchors. Last came the antenna cables. Hauling these heavy copper cables and pulling them taut was a prodigious task. It was all done by construction workers, many of whom climbed up the Ha'iku ladder each day. As construction progressed a cable car between the ground and the cable house at the top of the ridge made the task easier.

At last the five antennae were hoisted. Twelve-and-a-half-ton steel and concrete cable-pulls were required to hold them in place. The large concrete transmitter building containing generators and a 200-kw transmitter was complete. The station began transmitting in August 1943 and the system worked as intended. Signals were received as far away as Long Island and India, some 6,600 miles distant.

The Navy replaced the original wooden ladders with more permanent metal ladders in 1955. In 1957 the Navy decommissioned the unit as a communications facility. It was then used by the Naval Electronics Laboratory for research. By 1972 the long range radio-navigation OMEGA system was perfected, and the station was turned over to the U. S. Coast Guard. In 1971 new antennae were installed and the cable car operation dismantled. From that time on the stairs

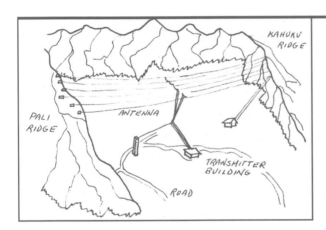

Transmitter building and antenna cables installed by U.S. Navy in Ha'iku Valley in 1942. The cables were removed in 1997 but the transmitter building survives and may be converted to a community center. (W. H. Dorrance)

were the principal avenue to cable anchor maintenance. A 2,800 foot climb could not be avoided, and the stairs were kept in reasonably good condition. The Coast Guard operated the transmitter as one of several Omega stations operated cooperatively by six countries worldwide.

Over the years, climbing the ladder became a challenge for intrepid O'ahu climbers and hikers. The Navy and then the Coast Guard made the ladder accessible to the public, providing that all logged in at the transmitter building and signed a waiver. It is estimated that as many as 20,000 climbers a year met the challenge of the ladder. All who made it to the top were rewarded with a magnificent 360-degree view of the island.

The climb was arduous. While the average inclination of the stairs was said to be thirty degrees, the figure is misleading. Some sections were almost horizontal followed by sections near vertical.

The stairs were metal and similar to those connecting decks on Navy vessels. There were exactly 3922 steps to the top.

The Coast Guard closed the ladder to the public in July 1987. It was announced that because of budget cuts, letting the public use the stairs was too much of a burden. Repairs and upkeep were too costly for the Coast Guard, and it was said that vandalism of the stairs had occurred.

A hue and cry from climbers has ensued. A group was formed dedicated to getting the stairs reopened to the public again. As of this writing (1998) it hasn't yet happened. However, City and State officials are on record as being in favor of reopening the stairs and national park status is being sought. Many would like to see the ladder ascent be perpetuated for future climbers. It's a fairly safe adventure, and there are few of those left.

Dr. John Ioworth Frederick "Fred" Reppun (1913-1995) was a throwback to an earlier time. He practiced medicine the way old-time country physicians used to: making house calls while keeping an office, charging minimal fees, and demonstrating a concern for the welfare and future of the community. Many a Windward O'ahu resident remembers Dr. Fred with deep affection. His story is a piece of Hawai'i's history.

PLANTATION DOCTOR

Windward O'ahu lost far more than a beloved family physician with the death of Dr. John Iwowerth Frederick "Fred" Reppun in 1995. Fred was a living, knowing repository of early twentieth century Windward O'ahu lore. During his early childhood he lived and grew up not more than 100 feet from his hillside home in Kahalu'u opposite Wailau peninsula. It was there that his father, Territorial and plantation physician Dr. Carl F. Reppun, raised his family. His son, Dr. Fred, held fond memories of those early days.

Dr. Fred Reppun started his practice in Hawai'i as a plantation doctor. Plantation doctors are a rare breed, growing rarer with each passing year, and such medical practice is unlikely ever to be repeated.

Dr. Fred graduated from Harvard Medical School and following internship and residency he was called into service with the Army

Medical Corps at the beginning of World War II. He left the Army in 1945 and, at age 31, he had never experienced the adventure of private practice.

Dr. Reppun longed to return to Hawai'i, but opportunities were scarce for young physicians. However, he learned of an opening as a junior physician with the pineapple plantation on Lana'i. He soon found himself backing up a senior physician who planned to retire once Fred had learned the ropes of medicine "plantation style."

Every morning the plantation clinic held sick call. The patients seated themselves on benches lining the walls of a large reception room. The doctor, closely followed by his nurse holding a clip board, stood before each patient in turn. After questioning, possible poking and/or stethoscopic listening, the physician turned to the nurse with a prescription which she recorded. Every patient got a prescription of some sort.

During his first such round accompanying the senior man Fred heard "ADT" being prescribed for one patient or another. In fact, it was the most frequent prescription. Fred had never heard of ADT before and thought perhaps it was a new wonder drug.

The two doctors retreated to the senior man's office after the last patient had been dismissed. "What's this ADT," asked Fred, "I never heard of that."

"Oh," replied his senior colleague, "didn't they teach you that in med school? ADT stands for any damn thing!" Like perhaps an aspirin or sugar pill.

Soon it was time for Fred to conduct sick call for the first time. He was a little anxious but after all, had accompanied the senior physician several times by then. He and the nurse entered the large reception room. It had its usual full house of pineapple workers and their dependents.

Dr. Fred approached the first patient in line on the bench, a gnarled, middle-aged field hand. He was Fred's very first such patient. "What seems to be bothering you?" asked the concerned young doctor.

Fred was speechless at the reply. "You the doctor. You tell me!" Fred learned not to use that question again.

Dr. Reppun was anxious to move on into private practice after five years of this. He learned that the only physician on Moloka'i was to retire and soon Dr. Fred Reppun was established there in private practice. It provided another five years of medical adventures "plantation style."

Fred travelled the island's rutted roads from one end to the other. It was a hazardous business then. He remembered that if it rained and you needed to reach one of the plantation houses in the village of Maunaloa, you risked getting stuck in the mud on the hill approaching the village. This road has since been paved but Maunaloa remains a plantation village in the process of being rehabilitated by Molokai Ranch.

Dr. John Iorworth Frederick Reppun (November 19, 1913 to March 15, 1995). Dr. Reppun retired from his Windward O'ahu practice in 1991. *(Reppun family)*

One of Dr. Fred's most poignant experiences happened on Moloka'i. He visited his patients more often than they came to him. After seeing one such large Native Hawaiian family several times, he gradually realized there was a mystery patient for whom he was prescribing that he never saw. He was determined to see that shadow patient.

Doctor Fred won the family's confidence and his mystery patient was presented. It was an elderly Hawaiian lady the family had been hiding away for all her adult life because they thought she was a leper. Fred examined her and determined that the poor soul was not leprous at all. She had a treatable skin condition that Doctor Fred soon brought under control.

It was on Moloka'i that Fred met a most serious medical challenge. A young pineapple worker was grievously hurt when a piece of heavy equipment overturned. He had serious internal injuries and would die without prompt attention. Doctor Fred concluded that he had to operate and soon. He was not a certified surgeon but none was available on the island.

Fred called a surgeon-colleague in Honolulu for advice. He responded, "Open him up and tell me what you see." Fred promptly did so after putting his patient under with what little anesthetic he had on hand. He described to his colleague what he found and they briefly discussed actions to take. Fred followed through, doing cutting and sewing. The healthy young worker was back on the job within a month.

Dr. Reppun never felt a need to purchase malpractice insurance in all of his years of practice (he retired from his Kane'ohe office in 1991). However, Windward O'ahu is full of Fred's patients who can testify to the fact that Fred always did fine.

CHAPTER SEVEN

Kane'ohe TO KUALOA

HE'EIA

THERE WAS A time not so long ago when fresh produce in the markets of Honolulu depended upon the tides at the shore in He'eia. Until Kamehameha Highway was paved through He'eia in 1922, the only way to reach the Pali Road from the farmlands north of He'eia was to drive along the beach in He'eia facing Kane'ohe Bay. It might take as long as a three-hour wait for the sea level to fall to the point where a farmer's model-T truck could make the passage toward the Pali Road after high tide. Then the farmer still faced another two or three hours of driving to and up the old Pali Road.

A good place to visit to learn about the ancient *ahupua'a* is Heeia State Park at the shore of Kane'ohe Bay on Kealohi Point, presided over by the Executive Director of Friends of Heeia State Park. At the park the visitor will find a gift shop stocked with items of Hawaiian history and lore, and a staff eager to inform visitors about He'eia.

He'eia Fishpond is now farmed for marketable seaweed by a preservationist and entrepreneur and operated as a commercial fish farm as recently as 1932. *(W. H. Dorrance)*

High Chief Abner Paki obtained title to the He'eia lands during the Great Mahele of 1848-1850. His daughter, Bernice Pauahi Bishop, inherited them upon his death in 1855. The title to the lands then passed to Bishop Estate when she died in 1884.

In the pre-Captain James Cook days (i.e. before 1778), He'eia Stream was lined with *taro* patches and drained through a floodgate-like arrangement into the eighty-eight acre Heeia Fishpond at the shore. For centuries the *taro* and banana harvests in the uplands were exchanged for fish caught in the bay and mullet grown in the fishpond, thus providing the natives with a balanced diet.

Heeia Fishpond is an engineering marvel built by natives lacking any of the tools and equipment of Western civilization. The pond is completely encircled with a four-foot wide stone wall that is some 7,600 feet long. As recently as 1932 the pond produced 100 pounds of mullet each day during harvesting season. The fishpond was designated a National Historic Site in 1973 when efforts to restore it were started. A preservationist and entrepreneur currently uses the pond to produce *limu* (seaweed) sold by several Honolulu markets.

From the mid-1800s until 1878 the dry lands of He'eia were given to ranching and roving cattle. Then John McKeague leased 2,500 acres and established his Heeia Agricultural Company. The plantation built a pier into Kane'ohe Bay so rail cars could move sugar out to coastal vessels that took it to Honolulu. Twice a week the *J. A. Cummins* picked up sugar and delivered supplies to the Heeia pier. The plantation's manager, George R. Ewart (1846-1927), served as chairman of the district's road commission from 1888 to 1890, and the district post office remained in the Heeia plantation settlement until 1912 when it moved to Kane'ohe. The plantation was closed down in 1903 and was the last sugar company to operate in He'eia or Kane'ohe.

Chinese rice paddies expanded in He'eia when sugar left. Rice flourished until about 1920 when California-cultivated rice made importing of Hawaiian-grown rice unprofitable. There were three rice mills in the He'eia-Kane'ohe locale during rice's heyday. One was located in the He'eia wet lands inland of the fishpond; another in Ha'iku Valley, and the third was a water wheel-driven mill at the shore. Mrs. Polly Ching, born in 1891, described it:

"[The mill]... was near the Waikalua River, and there was a ditch...that brought water from the river to make the water wheel go around...The Kane'ohe mill ground the rice of anyone who brought it to them...at that time everyone wanted to earn as much as possible and then go back to China."

Pineapple came to He'eia in 1910 when Libby, McNeil & Libby began leasing lands for planting pineapple in Kahalu'u, He'eia, Kane'ohe, and Kailua *ahupua'a* and built a cannery on Wailau Peninsula that operated until 1923. The lands were then abandoned to ranching, and later, residential developments.

During 1920 through 1922 Kamehameha Highway was paved from the Pali Road to Hakipu'u *ahupua'a*. The Long Bridge over He'eia Stream was completed in 1922.

Post-war developments in Kane'ohe and He'eia wiped out six fishponds lining the Bay that were filled to provide for 107 residential lots. A small fishing community called "Fish Camp" was replaced by the Alii Shores residential development. Never again would the men of Fish Camp take a taxi to deliver their catch to market in Honolulu. It's all a memory now.

When you continue this tour north on Kamehameha Highway 83, beyond He'eia you encounter an aging structure on the left. "Waiahole Poi Factory" reads the sign on the front. You have reached a unique place in rural O'ahu. Waiahole Valley is filled with glimpses of an older Hawai'i at its best.

The Poi Factory at the entrance to Waiahole Valley. The factory opens for business every Friday at 8 a.m. *(W. H. Dorrance)*

Usually the Poi Factory looks deserted. Looks are deceiving, however. The factory is the scene of industrious activity on Thursday and Friday mornings.

On Thursday farmers from within the valley and as far away as Kahalu'u bring *taro* harvests to the factory. These consist of the beet-like corms or tuberous roots. The factory converts the corms into *poi* using the cooperative labor of the farmers, friends, and neighbors. First the corms are washed of soil and stringy roots clinging to the tubers by immersing them in a large rectangular metal tank of water. Gathered around the tank are the workers. They reach in and massage the tubers to remove unwanted adhesions. The scene resembles a typical talk-story session of local residents at the beach, hanging over the sides of a pickup truck bed. A young woman with baby held in her left arm works with her right arm, her husband working nearby. Hawaiians, part-Hawaiians, *hapa-haoles,* and *haoles,* men and women, are all doing their part while joking, exchanging neighborhood gossip, and "talking story" in the Hawaiian way.

After being cleaned in the tank the corms are steamed to remove oxalic crystals that irritate the mouth. A large rotary press driven by an electric motor, similar to, but much larger than, the old potato masher, stands by to squeeze the corms into *poi.* The work goes on into the evening, and sometimes early morning, until the *poi* has been packaged in plastic bags for sales next morning (Friday).

Customers have arrived long before the factory opens for business. Parked cars and trucks line both sides of Waiahole Valley Road. It usually takes less than an hour to sell every bag of *poi,* such is its popularity among local residents. The building sometimes serves as a community gathering place, and on Fridays lunch is served to customers who enjoy authentic Hawaiian cuisine.

You should drive the length of Waiahole Valley Road if you feel you can spare thirty to forty-five minutes.

WAIAHOLE VALLEY

Waiahole Valley Road plunges deep into the valley and the visitor who proceeds inland is rewarded with some of the most beautiful, rural, and unspoiled scenery on O'ahu. Backed by the green Ko'olau Mountains, the foreground is filled with the rich greenery of banana plants, cultivated *taro* patches, papaya orchards, tended vegetable gardens, and homes graced with banyan and other species of trees. These are scenes of a Hawai'i of an older time.

As then, Waiahole Valley remains the home of perhaps fifty small parcel farming families. Centuries ago the *ahupua'a* of Waiahole was awarded to the *kahuna* as their lands for subsistence farming. This proprietorship was honored through the reign of Kamehameha I. During the last year of the Great Mahele of 1848-1850, commoners were awarded ownership of the land they occupied. Some fifty-three awards of less than ten acres each were made and several large plots were retained by the government and crown. The stage was set for today's land ownership.

Population in the valley has waxed and waned over the years but has never exceeded 1,000. In 1835-36, some 210 people lived in Waiahole Valley. By 1849 the number had dwindled to 127. At that time the population was mostly made up of native Hawaiians.

They were distributed among the small holdings devoted to *taro* farming located along the Auwai and the Waiahole Streams. This dominated the agricultural scene until about 1860 when Chinese began to purchase and lease *kuleana* for growing rice, and in 1879 constructed a mill. Rice was king in Waiahole Valley and by 1900 only 40 acres of *taro* remained. So it went until about 1920 when rice was finished as an export crop. Japanese farmers replaced the Chinese.

The growing of sugarcane that touched almost every cultivatable acre on the windward side of O'ahu at one time or another between 1860 and 1952 missed Waiahole Valley. The terrain of the valley is too rugged, marshy and wet for large-scale cultivation of cane. When sugarcane was being grown in nearby He'eia, Japanese farmers were raising crops of fruits and vegetables in Waiahole Valley.

Windward O'ahu has a resource of fresh water greatly coveted by the parched western, or leeward, side of the island. In 1913 an engineering feat was launched to divert much of this mountain water runoff to western O'ahu by means of a tunnel through the Ko'olau range. By 1918 the Oahu Sugar Company subsidiary, Waiahole Water

Company, had completed a system of ditches that collected mountain runoff and delivered it to the tunnel entrance at 750-foot elevation at the head of the valley.

The collected water ran down to the plantation's lands in 'Ewa where it was used to irrigate fields of the Oahu Sugar Company. When the company shut down in 1995, a dispute between Windward and Leeward interests arose over the distribution of this water. As of this writing (1998), interim agreements return much of the water to the Windward lands from which it was taken. Before this, the flow in Waiahole Stream was reduced to a fraction of its pre-tunnel value with a major negative effect on *taro* production.

The activities of the water company temporarily impacted on valley agriculture in a curious way. The company had constructed a ten-mile railroad through the valley to haul material to and from the shore of Kane'ohe Bay during construction of the water tunnel. Libby, McNeil, & Libby had constructed a pineapple cannery on the peninsula at Wailau Point. Hundreds of the drier acres in the uplands of the valley were planted in pineapple and for years the railroad hauled harvested pineapple to Waikane landing from which it was taken to the cannery by boat. Pineapple growing on Windward O'ahu proved to be unprofitable and by 1923 the cannery had shut down. Pineapple and the railroad disappeared from Waiahole Valley to be replaced by grazing cattle.

At the turn of the century the Territory appointed valley land-owner Lincoln L. McCandless (1859-1940) as forester. McCandless urged that the forests be fenced off and tree planting be done to replace the damage by foraging cattle. In 1918 the territory established the Waiahole Forest Reserve with 1,169 dedicated acres. By 1926 it had grown to over 3,000 acres by setting aside public and private lands.

Between 1937 and 1941 over 17,000 trees were planted in the reserve. The forests have been renewed and a valuable water conservation reservoir was restored. The north branch of Waiahole Valley Road ends at the edge of this dense forest.

The most exotic species planted in Waiahole Valley by the territory were twenty-seven acres of chaulmoogra trees in 1921. Chaulmoogra oil was used in the treatment of leprosy until the sulfa drugs were discovered. The grove flourishes to this day.

The Territory of Hawaii used Waiahole Valley to introduce many new species to Hawai'i. In 1928-29 and 1959 rainbow trout were planted in Waiahole Stream. One hundred tree frogs were released in the forest reserve in 1933. Then, in 1938, some 1,000 freshwater snails were turned loose in Waiahole Stream.

Developers threatened rural Waiahole Valley in the 1970s. There was talk of subdividing the valley and building golf courses and resorts. Buttressed by the public outcry of citizens throughout O'ahu, the families of Waiahole and neighboring Waikane Valley formed the Waikane-Waiahole Community Association to voice their protests. The state responded and in 1977 purchased 600 threatened acres from owner-developers. The state then announced its intentions to preserve the rural enclave and turn the acreage into an agricultural park and residential subdivision, preserving that which was already there.

Improvements came slowly to the valley. It wasn't until 1989-1992 that the rutted roads were rebuilt and substantial bridges constructed over the streams. In 1993, neighboring Waiahole Homestead Road residents finally got their distribution of potable water and electricity.

Community activism increased with the movement of younger people into the valley. Volunteer workers restored the Waiahole Poi Factory after several years of other uses. The factory is a living monument for one of O'ahu's most beautiful agricultural communities.

A few miles beyond the Poi Factory you enter the *ahupua'a* of Kualoa.

HISTORIC KUALOA

The land division of Kualoa is an enduring sentinel standing guard over the entrance to Kane'ohe Bay. The land is occupied by Kualoa Ranch and a spacious regional park. Visitors are rewarded with a vista of partly-forested plains meeting the ocean at Kualoa Beach, backed with a breathtaking view of Pu'u Kanehoalani, a ridge of the Ko'olaus. Mokoli'i Island (Chinaman's Hat) provides a counterpoint just 500 feet offshore. This fascinating place has a rich history.

Kualoa Regional Park is listed in the National Register of Historic places because of its importance to the Hawaiian people. Sacred Kualoa was a place of refuge and a location to which were brought the newborn children of nobility to be raised by foster-parents. Often, during the autumn *Makahiki* (an annual harvest festival, a time of peace lasting several months, celebrated with athletic competitions and religious observances), the priests of Lono, god of the *Makahiki,* began their tour around O'ahu starting at Kualoa.

Kualoa, with its neighboring divisions Ka'a'awa to the north and Hakipu'u to the south, was shown proper respect for traditions and the memory of chiefs who lived there in centuries past. All canoes lowered their sails when passing by. Hakipu'u *ahupua'a*, the southern neighbor, had been the home of Kahai, famous navigator who returned from Samoa with seeds and breadfruit. Kamehameha I, as late as 1795, showed respect for Kahai's memory by lowering the sails of his canoe off the coast of Hakipu'u.

High Chief Kahekili (1713-1794) of Maui preceded Kamehameha I in territorial ambitions and set out to extend his rule to O'ahu. In 1791 Kahekili established his court at Waikiki and pressed his son Kahahana, chief of O'ahu, to yield dominion over the sacred lands of Kualoa. Kahahana was reluctant and called a meeting of his chiefs and counselors to seek their advice. Samuel Kamakau tells of the outcome of this meeting in his book, *Ruling Chiefs.*

"...The kahuna [priest or expert] bowed his head, then, looking up, said, 'O chief! if you give away these things [the lands of Kualoa] your authority will be lost, and you will cease to be a ruler. To Kualoa belong the water courses of your ancestors, Kalumalumai and Kekaihehee; the sacred drums of Kapahuulu, and the spring of Ka'ahu'ula; the sacred hill of Kauakahi son of Kahoowaha of Kualoa. Without the ivory that drifts ashore you could not offer the gods the first victim slain in battle; it would be for Kahekili to offer it on Maui, and the rule would become his....Any other requests by Kahekili you might have granted, but not this...'"

Kahahana did not yield and it was left to Kamehameha I to thwart Kahekili's ambitions in a naval battle off northern Hawai'i in 1791, that was the first native engagement in which cannons were used by both sides. Kahekili retreated and died at Waikiki in 1794. Another son of Kahekili, Kalanikupule, became ruler of

O'ahu, and was later defeated by Kamehameha I in the epic battle of the Nu'uanu Pali.

In the Great Mahele, King Kamehameha III reserved the *ahupua'a* of Kualoa for himself. Scattered throughout Kualoa were some thirty-four *kuleana* of less than three acres that were granted to native Hawaiians, most along the shore. Kualoa remained a native Hawaiian place in the wake of the Mahele.

Dr. Gerrit P. Judd (1803-1873) was a medical man who had arrived in Hawai'i in 1828 with the third company of American missionaries. Possessed of enormous energy, Dr. Judd served until 1853 in the court of Kamehameha III in many responsible offices including minister of finance. In 1850 he purchased 627 acres in Kualoa from the king. It was to be the start of over 140 years of one family's ownership of Kualoa's lands.

In 1860, one of Dr. Judd's sons, Charles Hastings Judd (1835-1890), and a son-in-law, Samuel G. Wilder (1831-1888), occupied the Kualoa land with the intention of planting diversified crops. In 1865, in partnership with Dr. Judd, they planted sugarcane and built a steam-powered mill using the most modern machinery from Scotland. It was the first of its kind on O'ahu. However, by 1871 the mill was grinding the last crop of what was a failing venture. The land was just too dry and inhospitable for growing sugarcane. The mill's stone chimney can easily be seen from the highway.

In1870 Samuel Wilder gave up his dreams for Kualoa and deeded his share back to Dr. Judd. (Wilder went on to make his fortune in

Stone chimney of the former Kualoa plantation sugarmill that shut down in 1871. When built in 1865, the mill was the most modern on O'ahu. *(W. H. Dorrance)*

interi-sland shipping and in railroads he built on Maui and Hawai'i.) When Dr. Judd died in 1873, the lands of Kualoa passed to his son Col. Charles Hastings Judd, then Adjutant General of the Kingdom's modest military forces under King Lunalilo. Colonel Judd added to Kualoa lands purchased by his father in the neighboring *ahupua'a* of Hakipu'u and Ka'a'awa. Before his death in 1890, he had built the holdings to over 4,000 acres and started ranching operations.

Stewardship of the Kualoa and adjacent lands passed to Colonel Judd's daughter Julie (1860-1941). In 1887 she married the promising young Irishman Francis Mills Swanzy (1850-1917), destined to become minority owner and managing director of Theo. H. Davies & Company. She and Swanzy had two daughters, Rosamond and Nora.

Julie Swanzy was a force in the community in her own right and was very protective of the lands of Kualoa. She developed a portion of the beachfront as a private picnic and recreation area, and constructed a substantial stone bathhouse near the shore that stands, in a neglected state, to this day.

Something of Julie's nature is revealed by a story told about her. During the early 1920s the City and County of Honolulu was considering condemning the lands owned and improved by Kualoa Ranch on the ocean side of Kamehameha Highway in Kualoa (called "'Apua"), to make a public park where the Kualoa Regional Park is now located. Julie became very disturbed at the idea of a public park less than a mile from her home and resolved to do something about it. She asked Mayor John Wilson to join her on a drive to Ka'a'awa. During the ride Julie offered to give the City and County five acres of beach land in Ka'a'awa in return for their dropping the plans to develop a park in 'Apua. Mayor Wilson accepted her offer, thus establishing what is now called Julie Judd Swanzy Park and the nearby, smaller Ka'a'awa Park. The Kualoa beachfront lands were spared for a time at least, in Julie's eyes.

When she died in 1941 Kualoa Ranch was thriving with several hundred head of cattle, and ranching continues to this day under the stewardship of Dr. Judd's descendents. The lands he acquired in neighboring Hakipu'u included a large fishpond called Moli'i. Built before recorded history, the pond was worked more or less continuously into the early 1900s. In the 1920s Kualoa Ranch rented the pond to the Uemura family who lived near the pond and stocked it with 'awa(milkfish) and mullet. Their son, George Uemura, now rents and works Moli'i. The rich produce of the pond is sold at the fish market in Honolulu. Moli'i is one of very few Hawaiian fishponds that is commercially operated.

The steep slope of Pu'u Kanehoalani that borders Kualoa to the north is the location of long-disarmed coast artillery Battery Avery J. Cooper, named for an officer who died in 1944. In 1942 the Army engineers tunnelled deep into the mountain above the base of the cliff to emplace two six-inch guns. The guns hurled 105- pound armor-piercing projectiles to a range of 16 miles, and were positioned to sweep the entrance to the bay. The tunnels contained an electrical power plant, latrines, a galley, first aid and radio rooms, sleeping quarters, ammunition storage, radar apparatus, and a battery commander's station, and were protected from gas attacks with air locks.

Julie Swanzy did not live to see the formation of the public park she had avoided. It wasn't until 1971 that the City and County of Honolulu negotiated purchase of the land toward the ocean side of Kamehameha Highway. Today the public can use this broad and well-developed park where camping is permitted.

In 1972, in response to the growth of the visitor industry, Kualoa Ranch initiated its first trail rides for visitors, the beginning of its most visible enterprise. Horseback rides, swimming, water skiing, jet skiing, surfing, jogging, and just plain loafing in a picturesque rural environment are among the attractions offered to visitors.

The ranch incorporated as Kualoa Ranch, Inc. in 1980, and shares are distributed among descendents of Dr. Gerrit P. Judd. There are many children in the present, sixth generation, so it is likely that this *kama'aina* family business will continue for decades to come.

❖   ❖   ❖

It is clear from the forgoing that the Judd's are prominent in O'ahu's history. The patriarch of this family revealed a little of this during a recent interview.

PATRIARCH OF KUALOA RANCH

When Dr. Judd died, his will included the statement that "all cattle on the ranch bearing the brand 33 shall pass to inheritors with ownership of the ranch." Kualoa Ranch's present-day cattle brand was chosen sometime before 1873!

The number was taken for the simple reason that there were thirty-two ranches between Kualoa and the slaughterhouse in Honolulu. In those early days there were cattle grazing as close to town as Kahala, and it is easy to envision numerous herds scattered along the sparsely-settled Windward O'ahu coast.

The ownership of Kualoa Range passed from Dr. Judd's son, Charles Hastings Judd, to his daughter Julie Judd Swanzy. Her daughter, Rosamond Swanzy Morgan, mother of Francis Swanzy Morgan (b. 1919), took over management of the ranch in 1938.

As a young lad Francis Morgan spent summers and weekends at the ranch in the company of his mother. It was an exciting time when the ranch was almost exclusively dedicated to running herds of beef cattle and dairy cattle of several hundred head. Francis was enchanted by his mother's tales of "how it used to be."

One of Rosamond's stories told how the ranch periodically rounded up cattle to take them to the slaughterhouse in Honolulu. Late one afternoon the Hawaiian cowboys, often accompanied by her, and augmented by Hawaiian hired hands, would round up the cattle. Within an hour a herd of perhaps two hundred was assembled and driven down the government road (now Kamehameha Highway) to a holding pasture in Waikane on McCandless land where they were held overnight. The drive to the stockyards in Honolulu began early the following day.

Before dawn broke, the cowboys, sometimes including Rosamond, resumed the drive toward Kane'ohe. There they stopped for breakfast to fortify themselves for the arduous work yet to come. The cattle were driven up the Pali Road. (Imagine encountering a herd of cattle when driving along the then-narrow Pali Road!) After reaching the Pali Lookout about noon, the cattle were driven down Nuuanu Avenue to Wyllie Street, then west to the jungle in what is now called Shafter Flats opposite the slaughterhouse in Kapalama. Here the cowboys met their final challenge; preventing the thirsty cattle from wandering off in search of water in the brush and jungle.

Francis remembers helping ranch hands slaughter cattle under what was called "the slaughter tree," and processing the meat for local consumption. Such informal methods are forbidden today but it is interesting to note that in 1997 Kualoa Ranch contemplated constructing a modern processing plant on site, with the intention of marketing beef and other agricultural products to local consumers via a roadside stand. Kualoa Ranch beef is especially succulent because cattle are rotated among several pastures so that they continuously feed on fresh, green grass.

Francis was managing the ranch when World War II started. The Army abruptly moved in to build a landing strip and emplace weapons to protect the island from an anticipated Japanese invasion. A 6,000 feet long, steel-matted, runway was constructed that crossed the government road. A flagman held up traffic whenever aircraft (usually B-18 bombers and P-38 and P-40 fighter planes) took off or landed. This airstrip provided the basis for another of Francis' stories.

The Army parked aircraft for maintenance in two rows near the southern end of the runway, toward Kane'ohe. One day an officer sought Francis out and demanded he round up the half-wild cattle roaming the barracks area between the runway and the mountain ridge. Francis took some cowboys, drove the thundering herd down to the south end of the runway, then west toward Kane'ohe, intending to pen them up in Hakipu'u. His men forced the on-rushing cattle between the rows of aircraft being serviced by Army mechanics. "You never saw such a sight," says Francis. "There were soldiers running and scrambling in all directions!" He still chuckles at the memory.

After the December 1941 attack, Francis entered active duty Navy service. For fifteen months his official duties left time for him to manage the ranch part of the time. He saw the Army take more and more of the land leaving less for ranching. The Army continued to build structures and emplace weapons after he was called away for duty at sea.

Francis made a horseback tour of the ranch soon after his release from active duty in late 1945. The army's facilities were deserted and under the care of a single soldier-caretaker. Francis remembers dismounting near a shabby, brush-obscured, army building being lived in by the man and his young bride. He knocked at the door and was met by the terrified wife. She was sure she was being threatened by a wild west cowboy. No doubt an elderly lady lives today who remembers that long-ago innocent encounter with a real-life Hawaiian cowboy.

After considerable effort the runway was removed and the ranch restored to working condition. After 1972 trail rides and other attractions were added for visitors by Francis' children, Patricia, David, and John. Still, Kualoa Ranch remains a working cattle ranch perpetuating the proud tradition begun by missionary-doctor Gerrit P. Judd.

CHAPTER EIGHT

KUALOA TO LA'IE

IF YOU LOOK up to the left as you leave Kualoa you can catch a glimpse of the two large concrete canopies that protected the now-gone guns of Battery Cooper from rock slides. After you pass Ka'o'io Point on the right you enter Ka'a'awa *ahupua'a*.

FROM KUALOA TO La'ie

The stretch of Highway 83, Kamehameha Highway from Kualoa northwest to La'ie in Windward O'ahu, is sparsely settled but rich in legend, history, and park lands. Located in Ko'olauloa *moku,* this district contains fourteen ancient *ahupua'a* beginning with Ka'a'awa and ending at La'iewai. These *ahupua'a* contained no fewer than fifteen *heiau* in ancient times. However, eleven of these *heiau* have disappeared from today's maps. What have survived are several colorful settlements and oceanside parks, each with their own story.

Ka'a'awa is the first settlement entered proceeding north from Kualoa. Its history goes back through the time of Kamehameha I.

In 1804 Kamehameha was building strength on O'ahu in preparation for launching an invasion to conquer the island of Kaua'i. His army was organized under four wise and powerful high chiefs. Disaster struck in the form of deadly pestilence, brought to the islands by outsiders, against which the Native Hawaiians were helpless. The disease, called *ma'i oku'u* (the squatting sickness) by the Hawaiians, claimed the lives of Kamehameha's four key subordinates. One died in Ka'a'awa. Had these chiefs survived, wise men all, it is probable that the kingdom would have been stronger in the years following Kamehameha's death in 1819.

The Crouching Lion Inn is the next landmark encountered on the way north. Much of this rambling structure was built between

1926 and 1928 by George F. Larsen, a Honolulu contractor who arrived in O'ahu in 1912. It passed through other hands before being converted to an inn in 1951. While the location is known as "crouching lion" for the resemblance of the rock formation on the heights above it, the early Hawaiians knew the location as *Kauhi-imaka-o-kalani* (the observant cover of the heavens). There were and are no lions in Hawai'i.

Kahana Bay is next. Now the site of a beautiful park, in decades past it was the southern terminus of the 36-inch-narrow-gauge Koolau Railway Company. Nearly every unoccupied acre between Kahana Bay and Kahuku was at one time or another planted in sugarcane because of this railroad.

North of Kahana Bay is the small settlement of Punalu'u where David Makaliu Kaapuawa-o-Kamehameha (1898-1971) lived out his life. "David of Punalu'u" lived with his family in an authentic grass house that he constructed following the description of David Malo (1793?-1853), a Native Hawaiian historian.

The next settlement entered is Makao, said to be named for Macao, the small Portuguese-owned island close to Hong Kong.

Kaya's General Store in Punalu'u. This fine store was started by proprietors Mr. and Mrs. William Kaya following his service with the much-decorated 100th Infantry Battalion during World War II. Kaya is the son of a Waialua sugar plantation worker and the store is an excellent example of the diminishing number of picturesque rural O'ahu "mom and pop" enterprises. *(W. H. Dorrance)*

Missionary business agent Levi Chamberlain (1792-1849) recorded that the natives named the location Makao because trading ships from Macao took on provisions and cargo at this location.

John Carey Lane (1872-1958) was born at Makao on his family estate. The patriarch of the Lane family, William Carey Lane, a fiery man with Irish blood who had married a high-born Native Hawaiian, was intensely loyal to the monarchy. When the revolt against the

Republic was mounted in 1894-1895, Lane urged his three sons, a nephew and a friend to soldier in the revolutionary forces, which they did. The near-bloodless revolution was quickly defeated by Republican forces and the instigators were tried, convicted, imprisoned briefly, then most were pardoned.

John C. Lane went on to serve in the territorial senate from 1905 to 1907 and was instrumental in introducing the bill that created the City and County of Honolulu. He was elected mayor in 1914, and subsequently served as high sheriff of the territory until resigning in 1932.

Makao's northern neighbor, Hau'ula, was named for the proliferation of blooming *hau* trees scattered about the community. The beach park is inviting but the number of old trees has greatly diminished in recent years.

You pass Pounders Beach, a favorite body-surfing beach, before entering La'ie. For years property inland from this beach was owned by the Cecil Brown estate. Kaua'i-born Brown and his two brothers were prominent in the affairs of the Hawaiian Kingdom. In 1887 he was elected to the kingdom's House of Representatives and was instrumental in drawing up the constitution of 1887. Appointed the kingdom's attorney general in 1892, Cecil Brown subsequently ran for a seat in the House of Representatives from his rural district.

Cecil Brown's sister, Alice, married prominent merchant Herman J. F. Von Holt (1830-1867). His descendents maintained the beach-front property makai of the Brown estate and allowed public access. Recently the City and County of Honolulu purchased this land and turned it into a public park adjacent to Pounders Beach.

While driving north to La'ie you will follow the path of a common carrier railroad whose tracks once paralleled Kamehameha Highway, Highway 83. The story of this railroad is important to the history of Kahana Valley.

KAHANA VALLEY

Kahana Valley is the only publicly-owned *ahupua'a* in the state. Some twenty-six miles from downtown Honolulu, the 5,300 acre site of Kahana Valley State Park was established in 1970. Today, the thirty-one families living in the valley are committed to nurture and foster Native Hawaiian culture and spread knowledge of its values and ways. The Kahana *ahupua'a* is the last of the ancient land divisions that is unspoiled and accessible to the public. The park's development continues under the Park Manager of Division of State Parks.

Archaeologists tell us that Kahana Valley was one of the first areas settled by the ancient Polynesians over 1,000 years ago. The valley is ideally situated to support the cooperative subsistence style of living practiced by the ancient Hawaiians. Kahana Stream provided a steady source of water for upland *taro* patches. Huilua Fishpond at the shore provided abundant harvests of tasty mullet and milkfish. Schools of big-eyed shad periodically appeared within the reefs shielding the bay and were welcomed by native fishermen. It was impossible to starve in Kahana Valley.

The present-day residents of the valley (many with Native Hawaiian blood), are pledged to restore vestiges of this ancient way of life. Kahana Valley Park has become a "cultural-living park" because of their efforts. Visitors are encouraged to hike into the interior of the valley to enhance their understanding of early native life.

There are strong reasons why a considerable effort is required to restore vestiges of early native existence. The discovery of the islands for Europeans in 1778 by Capt. James Cook signalled the beginning of the end for traditional Native Hawaiian subsistence living. Word of his discovery spread and the islands endured visitors bringing venereal diseases, measles, mumps, poxes, and other ailments previously unknown in Hawai'i. By 1850 the native population was decimated and with it came a decline of traditional life. Kahana Valley suffered this loss along with other localities in the islands.

The Mahele of 1848-1850 had an adverse effect, too. Large parcels in Kahana Valley were acquired by *haole* owners with commercial interests at heart. The *taro* patches and fishponds fell into disuse. The situation was ripe for exploitation.

Pioneer *kama'aina* developer James Bicknell Castle brought change to the Valley when he chartered his Koolau Railway Company in 1905. It was Castle's grand dream to develop the Windward side of O'ahu in sugarcane and extend his railroad south from Kahuku. In 1909 Castle incorporated the Koolau Agriculture Company to farm his vast Windward O'ahu holdings. By then he had a stake in the Kahuku Plantation Company with its sugarmill.

Castle's Kahana Valley holdings were planted in sugarcane and his railroad hauled the harvests to the Kahuku mill. From 1905 until Koolau Agriculture Company shut down after World War II, residents of Kahana Valley consisted mostly of Japanese and Filipino sugarcane workers who lived in two separate camps. Revenues were lost when the Koolau Agriculture Company ceased operations, and by 1952 the railroad was out of business. Nothing remains of this railroad that never went beyond Kahana Bay. Kahana Valley became a neglected backwater occupied by the families of a number of Native Hawaiian fishermen, commuting workers, and squatters.

World War II interrupted this scene when the Army rented the valley for jungle warfare training of soldiers destined to move on to combat zones closer to the enemy. The Army built a coral-paved road into the interior of the valley. Other than this road there is little that survives beyond a few concrete bunkers located deep in the valley.

In 1942 three 5-inch guns were emplaced at the north side of the entrance to Kahana Bay that added to two large searchlights mounted on nearby towers. Nothing remains of this coast artillery armament and the Army returned the valley to the owners at the end of the war.

The beach at Kahana Bay is sandy, gently sloping, and is protected by an offshore reef. The beach was long recognized as one of the best in Windward O'ahu for swimmers and surfers. A forested picnic area is adjacent to the crescent of the beach. The awakening in the state to the importance of preserving one of the few unspoiled *ahupua'a* left led to the State's purchase of Kahana Valley and beach front in 1970. The valley is open, free of charge, to campers with permits, hikers on well-marked trails, and pig hunters in the highlands. Tours and demonstrations can be arranged for groups through the park's office.

The State recently implemented plans to extend the park's camping area deeper into the valley by moving the families currently occupying aging houses in that vicinity. Each of the thirty-one families signed a 65-year lease that allows them to occupy a house lot being developed by the State about one mile into the valley. In return for this lease each household will provide hours of volunteer service dedicated to reviving and restoring the ways of old Hawai'i. House construction began in late 1994 and low interest loans were made available to prospective occupants.

Participatory and interpretive programs being developed by park residents include gathering, preparing, and weaving *lauhala;* pounding *poi;* making useful things from *niu* (coconut); learning to use nets, traps, and lines; trying the old and new ways of fishing; learning ways to catch crabs; planting, weeding and harvesting *taro;* gathering ferns, buds, and flowers and making a *lei;* learning a *hula;* listening to folklore and legends; playing Hawaiian games; building a *hale* (house); and, after all that, resting, meditating, and enjoying peace and beauty.

Kahana Bay as seen from the entrance to Kahana Valley State Park. Hiking trails lead from the entrance about three miles into the interior of the valley. There are several picnic tables scattered under the trees next to the beach. *(W. H. Dorrance)*

Plans have been made to build traditional *koa* wood canoes for fishing the Hawaiian way. Given time, all of these activities will be available to organized groups by arrangement with the park manager.

Who knows? Maybe someday soon we will be able to participate in a community *hukilau* (fishing with a large net) at Kahana Bay. Canoes pulling a net in the bay will capture *akule* (shad) and other delectables. As the canoes draw near shore we will wade out to take over the task of pulling the fish-filled net into the shallows and on to the beach. There will be more than enough for all. Maybe some will go to the market in Honolulu. Just like in the old times.

Kahana Valley Park is also a great hiking area.

You enter the *ahupua'a* of Punalu'u as you leave Kahana Bay.

PUNALU'U

This beautiful Windward O'ahu *ahupua'a* has always been, and remains, a Polynesian place. Rich in history, the district even contains reminders of Hawai'i's monarchy.

Punalu'u was a lush land division occupied by Native Hawaiians pursuing a comfortable existence when the English explorer Capt. James Cook first visited Hawai'i. Banana and breadfruit cultivation took place in the upper reaches of the valley, *taro* ponds were terraced below, and succulent fish were plentiful in the ocean, there for the taking. The Hawaiians showed their appreciation for the bounties provided by the gods by constructing at least five *heiau* in the highlands of the *ahupua'a*. While post-Captain Cook rice and sugarcane cultivation erased much of the evidence, enough has survived to enable Bishop Museum archeologists to record it.

Around the turn of the century Chinese farmers moved into Punalu'u. Oriental plantation workers and residents in California consumed vast quantities of rice so the Chinese planted it where *taro* had been planted before. This crop disappeared when California-grown rice saturated the market. The disappearance was timely because grander plans were in the making for the fertile Punalu'u lands. James B. Castle hatched them. In 1905 he obtained a charter to construct his Koolau Railway Company narrow-gauge railroad eleven miles south from the Kahuku sugarmill to Kahana Bay. Then in 1909, Castle founded the Koolau Agricultural Company that planted sugarcane in the coastal plains as far south as Kahana. His railroad hauled harvests to the Kahuku mill for the next thirty-five years as Punalu'u became a plantation community.

In those early days the principal means of inter-island travel was by the coaster fleet made up of small steamers and sailing vessels. A pier located near the mouth of Punalu'u Stream was used to off-load and on-load freight. A rare break in the reef along that stretch of coastline allowed for safe approach to the pier. The pier disappeared with the coasters around the beginning of World War II.

Through all of this, there continued to be a Hawaiian presence. In fact, it included the descendents of Hawaiian royalty. That story begins in 1883 when King David Kalakaua proclaimed David Kawananakoa (1868-1908) and his two brothers, all of noble birth, as princes of the realm. In 1902 Prince David married Abigail

Campbell (1882-1945), daughter of wealthy businessman James Campbell (1826-1900). One of the several houses the Campbells owned was a fine home built in 1885 on the slopes of Diamond Head.

In the early 1920s this elegant house was barged to a spacious ocean side lot in Punalu'u. The 112-year old, well-maintained house now sits near the shore surrounded by a spacious lawn and gardens. Except for the cruel twists and turns of fate it might have become an ocean-side retreat for Hawaiian royalty. This house, along with two others along the Punalu'u shoreline, is owned by members of the Kawananakoa family.

Prince David's son, David Kalakaua Kawananakoa, known as"Koke," was a motorcycle-riding, free spirit in his youth. As told by Dr. Frederick Reppun, his father Carl ran a dispensary for the pineapple cannery once located on Wailau Peninsula between Kane'ohe and Kahalu'u. The narrow, newly-paved Kamehameha Highway ran between the dispensary and the peninsula. There was a poorly-banked turn in the highway just in front of the dispensary. One day Koke, probably on his way north to Punalu'u, roared into the turn in front of the dispensary while astride his motorcycle. Disaster struck when the motorcycle skidded onto its side and Koke went with it, losing an ear and fracturing a leg in the process.

Fortunately for him, Dr. Carl was present in the dispensary. Ten-year-old Fred remembered that his father found and sewed Koke's ear back on and set the fractured leg as good as new.

Not far from the Kawananakoa compound was the three-acre *kuleana* of David Makaliu Kaapuawa-o-Kamehameha, better known as "David of Punalu'u." He was fiercely proud of his Hawaiian heritage, and was the last Native Hawaiian to live out his life on O'ahu in a traditional Polynesian grass house. For fifty years, until his death, David tended his *taro* pond and plants with loving care while clad in the traditional *malo* (loin cloth). He became a tourist attraction as he was often seen policing trash on Punaluu Beach Park across the highway from his *kuleana*.

David and his school teacher wife raised two children in the native surroundings. It was a healthy upbringing and their children went on to a fine higher education. His son graduated from Harvard University and his daughter from the Church College of Hawaii, now known as BYU-Hawaii. Both became teachers and youth counselors. As for David, he died peacefully in his sleep in 1971 at the Hotel Hana on Maui while attending a Board of Education meeting with his wife. Don't look for David's "Nature's Kingdom" today. That which wasn't destroyed by the tsunami of April 1, 1946 has long been replaced with lush green overgrowth. It's all history now.

Of course these aren't the only Native Hawaiians populating Punalu'u. The Hanohano family constructed the Hanohano Hale high-rise condominium on their *kuleana*. They hold title to the land and building and receive rent from the occupants. The building has long been fully occupied and is conveniently situated near the shore.

A more recent arrival is Ahi Logan who opened Ahi's restaurant in 1997 at the location of the former Paniolo Cafe. Ahi, a *keiki-o-La'ie* (child of La'ie), like cousin and fellow-restaurateur Sam Choy, operated his business opposite the sugarmill in Kahuku for nine years until it burned down one night in June 1996. Ahi's new restaurant serves Hawaiian family-style meals and has become a popular Punalu'u lunch stop on the way north, as well as a place for satisfying dinner meals. It's a genuinely Native Hawaiian enterprise.

Driving northwest on Highway 83 after leaving Punalu'u you will arrive at the neat and thriving community of La'ie.,

La'ie

The Mormon community of La'ie is located on Windward O'ahu within the ancient *ahupua'a* of La'iewai in the *moku* of Ko'olauloa. La'iewai was heavily-terraced and under cultivation by Native Hawaiians for centuries before English explorer James Cook's arrival in the islands. In those early days at least two *heiau* were located within the *ahupua'a* signifying the presence and devotions of natives.

The *heiau* have not survived intact. Decades of sugarcane planting have taken their toll and only the vestiges of Nioi *Heiau* remain. The last of the terraces for *taro* planting were abandoned long ago and the remnants are overgrown and difficult to find.

In 1864 Brigham Young dispatched Francis A. Hammond and George Nebeker to Hawai'i to search out and obtain land for an agricultural colony. The *ahupua'a* of La'iewai was then owned by former U. S. Consul Thomas T. Dougherty and offered for sale to Hammond and Nebeker, who arranged a purchase. Nebeker returned in 1865 to serve as president of the mission and manager of the plantation from 1865 to 1873, when he was succeeded by A. F. Mitchell. Mitchell was barely installed in 1874 when King David Kalakaua and his Queen Kapi'olani (1834-1899), made the first of several visits to La'ie. The king was much impressed the tidy little community and was particularly pleased with the number of Native Hawaiian children. The kingdom was suffering from the dying-off of the native race in those times.

The development of the La'ie community owes much to The Church of Jesus Christ of the Latter Day Saints (followers of the Book of Mormon). Other notable leaders of the mission were Robert Noall, president and manager from 1892 to 1895, who strengthened financial management and did much to increase the community's water supply with wells and pumps, and Samuel Edwin Woolley, president and manager from 1895 to 1921, under whose direction the La'ie temple was constructed.

Sugarcane was cultivated on Laie Plantation beginning in 1872. It was a modest beginning. Only 200 acres were under cultivation in 1880, and the sugar product was shipped to Honolulu via schooner from a landing 1-1/2 miles south of La'ie at Pounders Beach. This mode of transport, along with the primitive mill, was a bottleneck to production until the Kahuku mill extended its plantation railroad to La'ie in 1896. At that time the Laie mill was abandoned and from then the Laie-grown cane was hauled to Kahuku. Production peaked at 4,830 tons of sugar produced in 1930. In 1931 the lands were sold to Kahuku Plantation Company and that company continued cultivation until the Kahuku mill shut down in 1971.

By 1879 membership in the Mormon Church in Hawai'i had increased to about one-tenth of the native population. A temple, said to resemble that at Salt Lake City, was to be built at La'ie. It was dedicated in November 1920 following years of construction. This fine church and the surrounding community are one of O'ahu's most popular tourist destinations.

The manicured campus of Brigham Young-Hawai'i, named for the founder of the Church, is located nearby. The school draws students from throughout the Pacific basin. This four-year university grew out of the former Church College of Hawaii, started at Laʻie in 1955, the name having been changed in 1974.

The Laʻie temple of The Church of Jesus Christ of the Latter Day Saints as seen from the approach parkway. *(W. H. Dorrance)*

One of Oʻahu's most visited tourist attractions, the Polynesian Cultural Center, located near the campus, opened in 1963. Many of the performers and guides in this well-designed attraction are students at the university. The center consists of a collection of mini-communities representing the way of life of South Sea island Polynesians and Melanesians. Visitors are treated to pageantry and can enjoy sumptuous meals in the center's restaurant. A visit provides much food for thought.

For years Laʻie has provided Oʻahu's visitors with memorable attractions. One was the monthly *hukilau,* a Polynesian community event. The group fishing expedition allows any and all to participate. The fishing men and women enter the water with a large net having a fine mesh bag in the center. The net's holding rope is festooned with *ti* leaves to direct fish to the bag. Other participants enter the water in front of the net to splash the water and scare the fish toward the net. A third group of participants on shore pulls the ends of the net while the net catches the fish. The Laʻie *hukilau* was started in 1947 to raise money to replace a burned-down chapel, and ended in 1970 because taxes were to be levied and the event couldn't sustain the added expense.

In 1908 James Bicknell Castle completed his Koolau Railway Company railroad south from Kahuku, through Laʻie, to Kahana Bay. While he died before extending the railroad further as he had planned, it opened the shoreline north and south of Laʻie to the building of country homes by prominent Honolulu residents. It was possible to travel from Honolulu to Kahuku via the O.R.& L. railroad and from Kahuku to La'ie via the Koolau Railway Company in less than a day's time when roads were primitive and automobiles were unreliable.

The Alvah A. Scott family was among the many prominent Honolulu families that built country homes near the shore south of La'ie. Scott served as president of Hawaiian Electric Company for a time and before that was Manager of Honolulu Plantation Company, Hilo Sugar Company, and an executive at C. Brewer & Company. In the late nineteenth and early twentieth-centuries much of the shoreline of La'iewai *ahupua'a* was occupied by prosperous *haole* families. It was a small and close-knit world now overtaken and obscured by development.

In 1993 Hawaii Reserves, Inc., a Hawai'i corporation, replaced former owner Zion Securities Corporation. Laie Water Company is owned by Hawaii Reserves. A master plan leading to the improvement of community facilities has been approved and Hawaii Reserves is dedicated to carrying it out. Today La'ie is an industrious community of 5,000 that can anticipate years of growth under Hawaii Reserves' well-constructed plan.

Chapter Nine

La'ie to Hale'iwa

Kahuku is the community furthest north on O'ahu.

Kahuku

IN JANUARY 1778 Capt. James Cook's *Resolution* and *Discovery* sailed by Kahuku on the way to dropping anchor off Waimea, Kaua'i. Lieutenant James King, one of Cook's popular young officers, recorded in his journal this description of Kahuku: "Nothing can exceed the verdure of the hills, the variety of wood and lawn, and the rich cultivated valleys, which the whole face of the country displayed."

Kahuku is one of thirty-four *ahupua'a* that make up the *moku* of Ko'olauloa. In Captain Cook's time the population of the entire district was less than 9,000 Native Hawaiians. Subsistence was a struggle because resources were few and scattered.

Haole civilization came late to Kahuku. In 1850 Charles Gordon-Hopkins started Kahuku Ranch following the Great Mahele. This property was acquired by Judge Herman A. Widemann (1822-1899) and Julius L. Richardson who, in turn, in 1876 sold a 15,000 acre parcel, including the ranch, to James Campbell for $63,500. The stage was set for what became Kahuku's major development.

Benjamin F. Dillingham had great plans for O'ahu. By 1889 his O.R.& L. railroad had been built beyond the Ewa plains and he contemplated extending it further beyond Ka'ena Point. In 1889 he leased Campbell's Kahuku lands for fifty years and subleased a portion to James B. Castle. Dillingham wanted the land developed in order to generate business for the railroad, and in 1890 Castle cooperated by organizing Kahuku Plantation Company. Castle planned to develop lands from Kahuku to Kane'ohe and this was his first step.

Kahuku Plantation Company planted cane on some 2,800 acres and erected a mill. The first crop was harvested in 1892 and by 1898 the plantation was producing 4,356 tons of sugar annually. The mill camp became Kahuku's first community. Construction of thirty miles of plantation railroad began in 1890.

For twenty-five years Kahuku held a distinction shared with no other Hawaiian locality because of the railroads. When James B. Castle chartered his Koolau Railway Company in 1907 Kahuku became the only locality in Hawai'i served by three railroads. Dillingham's O.R.& L. railroad extended from Kahuku around Ka'ena Point and down the west coast to Honolulu. The Koolau Railway Company railroad ran eleven miles south from Kahuku to Kahana Bay. The plantation railroad ran over the planted fields of Kahuku Plantation. This unique company triumvirate ended when the money-losing Koolau Railway Company railroad was absorbed by the Kahuku Plantation Company.

Kahuku was considered a small plantation, with less than 4,000 acres under cultivation. To make up for this, until 1931 Kahuku Plantation milled the sugarcane harvested at neighboring Laie Plantation owned by Zion Securities. In 1931 Kahuku Plantation leased the land from Zion Securities and added it to the acres leased from Campbell Estate. By 1935 the plantation was cultivating an additional 4,490 acres that extended as far south as Hau'ula.

The former Kuhuku Plantation Company sugarmill. The machinery in the mill house is the only exhibit in Hawaii of modern sugarmill apparatus and can be examined free of charge. *(W.H. Dorrance)*

In the mid-1930s most of the population of Kahuku worked on the plantation. The work force numbered 1,137 of whom 349 were U. S. citizens. The workers and their dependents lived in seven camps known as Main Village (265 dwellings), New Camp (39 dwellings),Camp 2 (17 dwellings), Camp 3 (16 dwellings), Camp 5 (16 dwellings), Hau'ula Camp, and La'ie Camp. All had recreational facilities, including lighted tennis courts. A plantation hospital was located at the Main Village as was a "talkie" movie with a 1930s admission of ten cents. A nine-hole golf course was available to all. At the close of 1935 the plantation's livestock included forty-nine horses and sixty-one mules used for field work.

In 1924 the Kahuku plantation became one of the first plantations in Hawai'i to replace the backbreaking *hapai ko* (lifting cane) work with mechanical lifting and loading. By 1938 the concept was being extended to mechanical harvesting and the sight of machete-wielding cane cutters disappeared forever soon after World War II.

Excitement came to Kahuku during World War II when the Army emplaced a battery of four eight-inch cannons between the mill and the shore. This battery could fend off any attempt to invade the island near that location. The Army establishment was augmented by a landing strip southwest of Kahuku that was kept busy during the war with the coming and going of fighter planes. By 1950 the fighter strip was abandoned.

Plantation life in Kahuku changed forever on November 31, 1971 when the plantation shut down. While younger employees found work with the state, city and county, and the new resort development at Kuilima, the older workers retired in the Main Village. Peaceful Kahuku entered a new era.

Fred and Joanne Trotter, Bud Morgan, and Wade McVay were determined to save the mill as a perpetual example of O'ahu's sugarcane heritage. They recruited Honolulu businessman Alan Beall who devoted himself to creating the Kahuku Sugar Mill development. The concept became a center of shops and restaurants located at the mill with its machinery preserved as a tourist attraction. Since 1972 the project has waxed and waned but today serves as a monument to the efforts of these industrious leaders.

Shoppers enjoy the variety of goods offered in the millyard shops, and the bar and restaurant, newly-renovated, draws the tired and thirsty. There is no other location in the islands where one can inspect at close hand the heavy machinery used to convert cane to sugar.

A particularly-historic piece of equipment stands in the yard before the entrance to the mill. There in painted splendor is a primitive three-roller mill that was propelled by animals, usually a yoke of oxen. This kind of mill was largely abandoned by 1870 and is unlikely to have been used at Kahuku.

Animal-powered sugarmill located in the mill yard fronting the Kahuku Sugarmill. The last mill in Hawai'i that used this kind of mill is believed to be the R. W. Meyer Sugar Mill located on Moloka'i that went out of business in 1895. *(W. H. Dorrance)*

Today's Kahuku is made up of a scattering of plantation retirees and younger people who have moved in to enjoy the "laid back" ambiance of Kahuku. The community takes great pride in the academic and athletic accomplishments of its high school scholars. The modern Kahuku Hospital serves the surrounding northern O'ahu communities.

In 1980 the U. S. Department of Energy erected an experimental wind-turbine generator in the hills southwest of Kahuku. Hawaiian Electric Industries formed a subsidiary, Hawaiian Electric Renewable Systems (HERS), to exploit the concept. From 1984 to 1993 HERS operated wind generators that generated one percent of O'ahu's electricity. A very large generator made by Boeing Aircraft Co. was recently installed and performs in an admirable manner. The two blades of this giant machine span 320 feet, turn at 15 to 18 rpm, and weigh 159 tons. After spirited bidding the wind farm was sold to New World Power Corporation which continues to supply electricity to Hawaiian Electric Company's power grid.

Leaving Kahuku behind, you will depart from Windward O'ahu and enter the region of O'ahu known as the "North Shore." It is widely-known for its surfing beaches, Waimea Bay being one of the first encountered after leaving Kahuku. The beauty of the beach at Waimea Bay is obvious to the eye but the story of the Valley beyond must be told to fully appreciate the locality.

WAIMEA VALLEY

This beautiful valley is located in Northwest O'ahu and straddles the border between Ko'olauloa and Waialua *moku*. The valley long enjoyed a sacred significance for Native Hawaiians. It was during the 11th century that the *ahupua'a* of Waimea was given to the *kahuna* of O'ahu to be held by them in perpetuity. This award was respected through the reign of Kamehameha I and was held by his *kahuna nui* (preeminent priest), Hewahewa, until his death in 1838. By then the religion of *kapu* (iron rules) was largely displaced by Christianity and the *kahuna* lost their significance and influence.

The priests and their followers constructed at least three *heiau* in and bordering the valley. Pu'u-o-Mahuka Heiau, on the ridge north of Waimea inlet, is the largest *heiau* on O'ahu and is thought to have been the location of human sacrifices. Kupopolo Heiau is on the opposite ridge of the valley, and in 1974 the smaller Hale-o-Lono Heiau was discovered back in the valley. Carbon-dating of coral used in its construction revealed that it dates from between the fifteenth and eighteenth centuries.

Waimea Valley is the location where Europeans first set foot on O'ahu. Following Capt. James Cook's death at Kealakekua, Hawai'i in February 1779, his ships the *Resolution* and *Discovery*, set sail to continue explorations. Intending to return to Waimea, Kaua'i for reprovisioning at a location where they had been hospitably received earlier, the ships sailed along the northeastern coast of O'ahu. Taken by the inviting beach at Waimea Bay they dropped anchor off shore.

It is remarkable that they should venture ashore at previously-unvisited Waimea, O'ahu, considering the strife that they had so recently encountered at Kealakekua. Nevertheless Capt. Charles Clerke (1743-1779), successor to Cook as commander of the expedition, went ashore with a few men to examine the area. Their observations are recorded in the description of Cook's voyages as written on the expedition's return to England:

"...The sight of a fine river, running through a deep valley, induced us to come to an anchor in thirteen fathoms of water with a sandy bottom...the mouth of the river bearing southeast half east, one mile distant....We were much disappointed to find the water had a brackish taste, for two hundred yards up the river, owing to the marshy ground through which it empties itself into the sea. Beyond this, it was perfectly fresh and formed a fine running stream, along the side of which I walked until I came to the conflux of two small rivulets that branched to the right and left of a remarkably steep and romantic mountain. The banks of this river, and indeed of the whole we saw of the northwest part of O'ahu, are well cultivated and full of villages; and the face of the country is uncommonly beautiful and picturesque."

Except for the cultivation and villages, this description could be used today to describe Waimea Valley. (Captain Cook's ill- starred successor, Capt. Charles Clerke, died at sea of tuberculosis in August 1779.)

Waimea Valley continued to be the location of villages and *taro* cultivation into the nineteenth century. In 1898 the old ways were destroyed by a disastrous flood that wiped much of the valley clean. The native community never fully recovered. Today Waimea Valley is the site of a rich variety of ancient Hawaiian artifacts carefully preserved for the visitor. Bishop Corporation acquired the valley in 1969 with the intention of restoring and preserving the valley's rich history. The corporation's Waimea Valley Park is the enterprise that protects and maintains the evidence of a Native Hawaiian past. A place was created that includes a fine botanical garden and authentic Hawaiian entertainment and recreation.

In 1974 Bishop Museum archeologists found and identified the site of Hale-o-Lono Heiau. For the next ten years Waimea Park historian Rudy Mitchell worked to restore the *heiau* to its original appearance. Today, because of Mitchell's devotion, it is possible to view an ancient Native Hawaiian *heiau* in its original configuration, including the thatched housing for sacred drums, an oracle tower, a storage tower for sacrificial objects, a replica of a typical carved wooden statue, and the refuse pit in which human remains were disposed. A *heiau* was far more than a carefully-assembled pile of stones.

Waimea Valley Park is an example of how profit-seeking and conscientiousness have combined to preserve Hawaiian history.

❖   ❖   ❖

It is difficult to find a tie between the isolated Hawaiian Islands and a seaport of the newly-formed United States in the late eighteenth century, but nevertheless the tie is there. The story of this tie is an obscure piece of O'ahu's history.

THE NORFOLK CONNECTION

Only by the wildest stretch of the imagination could Waimea Valley on O'ahu's North Shore be coupled with the bustling East Coast seaport of Norfolk, Virginia two hundred years ago. In 1791 when O'ahu was four years away from being incorporated into Kamehameha I's grand scheme for a Hawaiian Kingdom, the Commonwealth of Virginia was in its eighth year as a member of the newly-formed United States.

In that same year, Englishman George Vancouver received His Majesty's instruction to proceed with a Royal Navy squadron to complete the explorations of the Hawaiian Islands and Pacific Northwest begun earlier by the ill-fated Capt. James Cook. Vancouver had served as a seaman, then midshipman on Cook's second and third voyages, and surely knew as much about the remote territory as any English naval officer.

The Admiralty supplied Vancouver with three ships for the explorations. The vessels *Discovery* and *Chatham* formed the exploring squadron. Converted ship of the line *Daedalus* was to be a supply ship and would meet the others at least twice during the extended voyage for purposes of resupplying the explorers. The squadron left Portsmouth, England full of hopes for finding the long-sought (and imaginary) Northwest Passage across North America, and for cementing England's claim to a piece of Oregon territory ceded to Britain earlier by the Spanish. It was to be three years of adventure.

Daedalus, commanded by Lieutenant Hergest of the Royal Navy, connected with the advance two-ship party near the Hawaiian Islands. She undertook to explore the islands independent of the others after resupplying them. It led to disastrous consequences.

By 1792 *Daedalus* was sailing along the North Shore of O'ahu when her officers were taken by the beauty of the coastline. The captain, Lieutenant Hergest, decided to drop anchor off Waimea Valley and go ashore. He took one of the ship's boats through the reef and landed on the broad, semi-circular expanse of beach. He left an armed party to guard the boat and proceeded into the valley with his astronomer, a man named Gooch, and two seaman.

The *ahupua'a* of Waimea had been ruled by *kahuna* since the exclusive award to them made decades before by the king of O'ahu. The *kahuna* were aided in protecting their dominion by a band of fierce tattooed warriors. The deadly nature of the *haole* muskets and gunpowder was well-known to the envious *kahuna* and warriors, and they were determined to acquire some for themselves. They attacked Hergest and his companions and killed them. They then attacked the terrified boat guards and seized their muskets. The warriors forced the boat back to *Daedalus* and retreated into the valley where, it is thought, the bodies of Hergest and his men were offered to their gods.

A year later found the *Daedalus* rounding Cape Horn and beating its way north along the eastern coast of South America on its long voyage home. Depending on winds and sea conditions, the

View overlooking Pu'u o Mahuka Heiau toward Ka'ena Point in the distance. The *heiau* is located on the bluff that forms the northeast side of Waimea Valley and is believed to be the location where the bodies of Lt. Hergest and his two shipmates were left to appease the gods. *(W.H. Dorrance)*

voyage could consume the better part of a year. Stops were made at friendly ports for reprovisioning and refitting along the way.

Determining whether a port was friendly was a hazardous undertaking for *Daedalus* at this time. In 1793 England was making war on France. In wouldn't do for an English ship like *Daedalus* to anchor in a French-controlled harbor. The captain of *Daedalus* concluded that it would be best to find shelter in a United States harbor despite the risk that hostility of the Americans toward Great Britain was strong.

So it was that the unfortunate *Daedalus* sailed into the entrance of Chesapeake Bay and anchored off Norfolk town. The waters off Norfolk were crowded with several French vessels. A French agent, one Moreau, recorded that the appearance of *Daedalus* "creates a delicate and dangerous situation for that town [Norfolk], which nothing can remedy so effectively as its [the town] being put in a state of respectable defence. Indeed information has been received by which it would appear that the *Daedalus* had fired a shot in a very unjustifiable manner."

If the touchy *Daedalus* fired a shot it might be understandable, given the unfriendly treatment received during its voyage. The town of Norfolk was not happy to see *Daedalus* off shore. After all, the French had recently aided the Americans against the British during the Revolution, and American sentiments favored the French now that France and England were at war.

The United States had constructed Fort Norfolk to protect Norfolk Harbor. In 1794 the fort was manned by a motley crew of ragged militiamen eager to display their bravado. What better way than to sink a British ship?

Daedalus had foolishly anchored well within cannon shot. She was a tempting target for the American gunners as they plotted their attack. Even the poorly-trained volunteer American gunners could hit such a target.

So it was that on the night of May 8, 1794 *Daedalus* received three balls fired by the cannon from nearby Fort Norfolk. Damage was minimal but the point was well made. The ship was not welcome in Norfolk Harbor.

Daedalus lost no time in hauling anchor and limping for home following the attack. One can well imagine the tales told to wives and sweethearts upon arrival at Portsmouth. The survivors of the long voyage had every reason to say, "It's a very unfriendly world out there."

The voyage of *Daedalus* left unpleasant memories with Native Hawaiians. Captain Vancouver was outraged when he heard about the murder at Waimea Valley and demanded that the perpetrators be punished. Kahekili, ruler of O'ahu, Moloka'i, and Maui at the time, seized three unfortunate natives, who may or may not have participated, tried them and found them guilty, and had them executed with a pistol shot to the head while in a canoe alongside Vancouver's *Discovery* at anchor off Waikiki. It was a very unfriendly world out there for all concerned. "Daedalus" in Greek means "the cunning worker," surely a misnomer for the unfortunate frigate.

Kawailoa is one of the last sugar plantation camps surviving on O'ahu. As of 1997, it was scheduled to be demolished after the retiree-residents transfer to the mill camp located behind the inoperative

Waialua sugarmill or to other locations. A side trip to view Kawailoa does much to reveal plantation living as it used to be.

KAWAILOA

Kawailoa (long waters) takes its name from the lengthy gulch and waters of the Anahulu River, said to be the longest river on O'ahu. Originally, Kawailoa was the name of a *ahupua'a* within the *moku* of Waialua. The boundaries lost their official usage after the Great Mahele of 1848-1850 and those names of *ahupua'a* that survive are associated with communities and not the original land divisions. So it is with the plantation village of Kawailoa.

The original Kawailoa extended from the shore to the ridges of the Ko'olau mountain range. It was one of the largest *ahupua'a* within Waialua *moku*. *Taro* patches lined the river and streams in the uplands. Mullet and other delicious fish were cultivated within two large ponds near the shore. It was a hospitable location for Native Hawaiians following a subsistence way of life.

Puena Point is located at the shore midway between the eastern and western boundaries of the ancient *ahupua'a* and is the site of several ancient artifacts. A place on the point called Maeaea is said to have been the place where the body of a beloved chief was left to decompose after he was killed during an unsuccessful uprising against Kahekili, then ruler of O'ahu.

A *heiau* located on today's maps is a testimony to the density of the native population ancient times. One of the two fishponds was worked as recently as the 1930s but both are now abandoned to weeds and silt.

In 1898, Castle & Cooke established the Waialua Agricultural Company (later Waialua Sugar Company) on leased and purchased land. The plantation was divided into the sections of Halemano, Waialua, and Kawailoa for management purposes. For efficiency's sake field workers were housed in camps located close to their fields. Today's Kawailoa is one of these camps that survives.

While the camp was located amidst sugarcane fields it was not totally isolated from the outside world. One of the main spurs of the plantation's railroad ran to and beyond the camp. Many a ride was hitched on a canehaul rail car. As for travelling further, the O.R.& L.

had a scheduled stop on the timetable marked "Kawailoa." The boarding platform was located about a mile from the camp towards the shore. Honolulu was a little over two hours away riding the O.R. & L.

Until the labor strike of 1946, camp life was predictable and uneventful. All workers earning $100 or less per month received medical care free of charge for them and their dependents. The plantation maintained a hospital at the mill and a trained nurse made regular weekly calls at every camp. Each had a meeting house and recreational facilities. An inter-plantation baseball league was popular for decades. A beach reserved for plantation workers and dependents was located at Pu'uiki.

The sugar industry was determined to do what it could afford to continually improve housing for the workers. In the 1930s the industry's Hawaiian Sugar Planters' Association helped meet the demand by turning out standard designs for two and three-bedroom houses having every amenity. In 1935 Kawailoa's houses were replaced with these newly designed homes and they survive to this day. Several families, about half retirees, now occupy them. The sugar company maintained the houses but Bishop Estate owns the land. Each family paid $42 per month rent. Water and electricity were separately billed.

World War II brought excitement to Kawailoa camp. Concerned about the relatively open North Shore, the Army rushed to emplace large guns at strategic locations to ward off any invasion attempt.

Coast artillery command and fire control station located in Kawailoa. This four-story concrete structure was constructed in 1942 and appeared briefly in the movie _Picture Bride_. (W. H. Dorrance)

After the December 7, 1941 Japanese attack, a four-gun battery of 155-mm field guns was rushed to Kawailoa to be located within a mile of the camp in an northeasterly direction towards Kahuku. At the same time a battery of four eight-inch caliber railroad guns was located on a special railroad spur about one mile southwest of the camp toward Hale'iwa. Several powerful searchlights were mounted on tall towers along the shoreline. Nothing remains of these military emplacements.

There is something of this effort that does remain, however. About one-quarter of a mile from the camp on a plantation road leading northeast from the *luna's* (foreman's) office in the camp is a curious rectangular, four-story concrete structure that appeared briefly in a scene of the movie *Picture Bride*. Still faintly bearing World War II camouflage paint, it served as a fire control station and command post for all Coast Artillery soldiers manning the guns guarding the North Shore.

In 1994 Dole Food Company announced that it would close the plantation down in 1996 after years of loss-ridden operations. Some Kawailoa residents thereby lost jobs and all faced an uncertain future. In 1997 it was announced that Kawailoa camp was to be demolished after all retiree residents had moved to houses in the Waialua mill camp. Non-retirees were granted time to locate residences elsewhere. Soon all vestiges of Kawailoa will be gone forever along with the lush green sugarcane fields.

Hale'iwa is the next North Shore town.

The road through town takes you past the many plantation-town storefronts that give Hale'iwa much of its charm. Several restaurants are located along the road through town and it's a good place to stop for lunch.

"The bridge you love to hate". This narrow two-lane bridge crosses the Anahulu River at the entrance to Hale'iwa town. *(W. H. Dorrance)*

Visiting Hale'iwa

A visitor to the North Shore community of Hale'iwa is struck by the vibrant, busy, and cosmopolitan selection of small businesses that have captured the town. A smattering of artists, surfing equipment impresarios, slow and fast-food restaurants, shave ice, tee shirt merchants, and other colorful enterprises have sprouted in what was once a typical plantation town. Despite all, it is apparent that a conscientious effort has been made to preserve the town's architectural heritage and that is what makes Hale'iwa so special. The many funky storefronts suggest how it was in the recent past.

What was, and is, was determined by Congregationalist missionaries, a railroad baron, sugar plantation tycoons and workers, a plucky group of small-store entrepreneurs, and modern-day business people.

In 1832, when the newly-arrived Reverend John S. Emerson (1800-1867) and wife were dispatched to Waialua *moku,* they settled on a plot of land north of, and near, the mouth of the Anahulu River.

The Emersons were greeted by dispirited Native Hawaiians who were beaten down by decades of labor enforced by their chiefs. The lush upland forests of sandalwood trees had been harvested by them while they neglected the agricultural pursuits so necessary to customary subsistence living. The Emersons provided a spiritual regeneration. He and his wife Ursula travelled widely and preached to a flock as far south as Ka'a'awa and west to Wai'anae. They founded the Waialua mission on arrival and a mission school in 1839. In 1832 a church building, the replacement of which is still standing and later named for Queen Lili'uokalani, was built. John and Ursula served the mission until retirement in 1864 and spent the rest of their days at their Anahulu River home. The Waialua mission led to the next development for what was yet to be known as Hale'iwa.

In 1865 missionary son Orramel Hinckly Gulick (1830-1923) arrived to establish a school for native girls. A school compound, the Waialua Female Seminary, was built across the Anahulu River from the Emerson home. In time the school was informally called Hale-Iwa taken to mean "beautiful home" after the nest of the iwa bird. (A mistaken belief, as the nest of the iwa or frigate bird is far from beautiful.) This was the earliest known use of Hale'iwa to describe the locality.

Hale'iwa's Queen Lili'uokalani Church. This church replaced the original church constructed at the site in 1832. *(W. H. Dorrance)*

Alas, the seminary did not survive. The dilapidated building closed when long-time headmistress and missionary daughter Mary Green retired in 1882 due to declining health. Hale'iwa had gained a name and lost an institution.

Enter the railroad baron. In 1878 Benjamin F. Dillingham was granted a charter by the kingdom to build a railroad to serve the western and northern districts of O'ahu. He built his narrow-gauge O.R.& L. line from Honolulu to as far as Kahuku by 1899. Passenger service to and from remote Kahuku and Waialua was unlikely to be heavy when limited to plantation workers and infrequent North Shore visitors. Dillingham saw that steady fares would be generated for his railroad if he could make the area near the mouth of the Anahulu River a popular resort area. He anticipated those who built resort hotels on Waikiki Beach by years when he built the Hale'iwa Hotel. The sumptuous resort hotel, designed by prominent architect Oliver G. Traphagen, opened in 1899.

Dillingham did his best to make a visit to Hale'iwa memorable. He employed the distinguished Native Hawaiian Col. Curtis P. Iaukea (1855-1940) as the hotel's first manager. Colonel Iaukea supervised the furnishing of the elegant establishment. Then, to reinforce the railroad traffic to Hale'iwa, the O.R. & L. scheduled regular Sunday excursion trains from Honolulu. For years a $2.00 fare would purchase a pleasant day spent in Hale'iwa. The railroad journey between Honolulu and Hale'iwa took about two hours.

Waialua plantation workers passed through the small community adjacent to the hotel when travelling between the mill camp in Waialua and the plantation camp in Kawailoa on the Kahuku side of Hale'iwa. Early plantation workers, predominately Japanese, saw a business opportunity in this traffic and in servicing the swells who visited the hotel. When their work contracts expired many opened stores in Hale'iwa. The years between 1900 and 1941 were years of growth, prosperity, and stability for the merchants in Hale'iwa.

Original H. Muira Store located on Kamehameha Highway, Hale'iwa's "Main Street" looking northest toward Kahuku. The Muira Store is one of many original plantation town stores lining Hale'iwa's main street. *(W. H. Dorrance).*

The war years from December 7, 1941 to mid-1945 were a time of excitement. A runway constructed next to Haleiwa Beach Park was used by Air Corps fighter planes, and the Army took over the Haleiwa Hotel for officers' quarters. The Hale'iwa airstrip earned a permanent place in O'ahu's history when, in the midst of the December 7, 1941 attack, 2d Lt. George M. Welch and 2d Lt. Kenneth M. Taylor stationed at Wheeler Field took off from the airstrip in their P-40 fighters and engaged the enemy. The two pilots accounted for downing at least six of the attacking Japanese aircraft.

The tsunami of April 1, 1946 wiped out several sections of the O.R. & L. tracks and the railroad permanently closed down in 1947. The hotel closed soon after and was demolished by 1952. For a time Hale'iwa languished as a sleepy plantation town.

Statehood came to Hawai'i in 1959, followed by jet transports. The tourist industry and the popularity of the North Shore surfing beaches combined to regenerate Hale'iwa. The new entrepreneurs who have occupied Hale'iwa have done much to preserve the village's architectural heritage.

CHAPTER TEN

HALE'IWA TO DOWNTOWN HONOLULU

WAIALUA MOKU

THIS AREA STRETCHES from Waimea Valley at the eastern end to Ka'ena Point at the western end. The Wahiawa District forms the inland or southernmost border. The boundaries of Waialua *moku* were established over four centuries ago by the ruling chief of O'ahu and survive intact to this day as the boundaries of a judicial, tax, fire protection, police, and civil defense district. Before the Great Mahele the *moku* was divided into fourteen *ahupua'a*. Today the district's population is mostly gathered in the communities of Waialua, Hale'iwa, Mokule'ia, and Kawailoa. It wasn't that way in the beginning of Native Hawaiian occupancy.

Waialua *moku* was the site of one of the earliest settlements by Hawaiians. The fishing was bountiful, the land hospitable to healthy growth of breadfruit, *taro,* and bananas, and the slopes were covered with a rich canopy of trees including sandalwood. It all changed about 1810 when visiting American traders discovered the abundance of the sandalwood, a fragrant wood much in demand in China. Waialua *moku'*s forests were burned to expose the aromatic sandalwood, which was then harvested by Native Hawaiians to the neglect of their fishing and agricultural pursuits. Only the kings and *ali'i* benefited from this tragic activity.

Levi Chamberlain, who had arrived earlier with the second company of missionaries, travelled far and wide throughout O'ahu inspecting the schools. He noted the rich and neglected lands of Waialua *moku* in his travels. Two of his sons, Warren and Levi, Jr., remembered Levi's observations when, in 1864, they launched a sugar-making operation in Waialua District on family-owned acreage. It was during the Civil War when Hawai'i-produced sugar enjoyed a temporary prosperity because the northern states were cut off from sugar produced in the southern states of the fractured union.

The prosperity ended after the Civil War in 1865, and Warren and Levi Chamberlain surrendered control of the plantation to the bankers about 1870. Finally, in 1875, the struggling plantation was sold to pioneer grower Robert Halstead (1836-1900). He and his two sons ran the small and isolated plantation in the name of Halstead Brothers. Product and supplies were shipped and received by coastal steamer. Sugarcane farming in the Waialua District was about to blossom on a large scale when Robert Halstead died in 1900.

It was railroad tycoon Benjamin F. Dillingham who did the fertilizing that led to the blossoming. Dillingham had extended his O.R.& L. railroad to Kahuku and needed freight revenues. The Halstead plantation was too small to generate the revenues needed, so Dillingham persuaded Castle & Cooke to take control of the plantation and enlarge it. In 1898 Castle & Cooke formed Waialua Agricultural Company, with Halstead's lands, purchased or leased the surrounding small parcels, erected a modern mill, and began large-scale sugarcane farming. The appearance of Waialua District was determined for the next ninety-seven years when the missing canopy of trees was replaced by well-tended, lush green fields of sugarcane.

Castle & Cooke's Waialua Agricultural Company plantation became one of the three or four largest producers in Hawai'i. During its heyday, in the mid-1930s, the plantation was cultivating sugarcane

Now-dormant Waialua plantation sugarmill closed down in 1996 after ninety-eight years of operation. (W. H. Dorrance)

on 10,500 acres and milling additional cane grown on some 500 acres by independent growers. About 1,700 workers were employed who lived with their dependents in company-owned houses located in the several villages or "camps."

A sugarcane farm and mill is a dusty and dirty establishment whose appearance does little to suggest the highly-efficient industrial plant that it must be to survive. Looks are deceiving, however. A

Waialua mill camp house of 1935 HSPA design. Plantation retirees were being transferred from Kawailoa Camp to the mill camp starting in 1997. It was planned that Kawailoa camp be demolished when all the Kawailoa Camp houses are vacated. *(W. H. Dorrance)*

Hawai'i-based sugar plantation and mill is the most efficient farming and milling operation that engineers can devise.

Transportation costs for hauling the harvests to the mill were immediately reduced by Castle & Cooke when a plantation railroad was installed to replace the oxen and mules that hauled cane for the Halsteads. Then, with the perfection of heavy-duty, diesel-powered trucks, costs were further reduced when Tournahaulers replaced the railroad in 1952.

Vast improvement in crop yield occurred with the installation and improvement of the irrigation system. The 2,544-million gallon Wahiawa reservoir that was constructed added to the storage capacity of over twenty smaller reservoirs scattered around the plantation. Additional irrigation water was supplied by several high-capacity pumps that raised ground water from wells. The water was distributed to the fields using a carefully-designed schedule. A hydroelectric plant driven by water draining from the Wahiawa reservoir delivered electricity to run the pumps and supply the camps. Eventually, aircraft were used to spread fertilizer. Loading cane by hand onto the cane haulers was replaced first by mechanical derricks and then by hydraulic grabs. Everything that can be mechanized is mechanized. Sugar workers are proud of their production and accomplishments.

In 1985 the plantation was purchased by financier David Murdock and renamed Waialua Sugar Company, division of Dole Food Company. The management of the plantation was combined with that of the Dole Pineapple Company in 1993. The plantation was losing money and in 1995 it was announced that it would close down. In 1996 a colorful era ended forever in Waialua *moku.*

Plantation retirees were transferred from their homes in Kawailoa to vacated houses in mill camp starting in 1997. The retired plantation workers and dependents were guaranteed housing for life as a condition of employment and the company is keeping its word. No guarantee was made that the venerable mill camp general store would be maintained, however. In July 1997 one of O'ahu's last plantation stores, Fujioka's Store, closed, a victim of the declining local economy brought on by the shutting down of the plantation.

Mill camp is one of a very few surviving plantation communities on O'ahu. The streets are neatly laid out in a rectangular grid but are rutted and unpaved. Ancient corner street signs identify each street.

Fujioka's Store before it was closed down in July 1997. This prototype plantation camp store was located in Waialua Mill Camp behind the sugarmill and was representative of plantation stores of bygone days. The building still stands. (*W. H. Dorrance*)

Most of the houses are in good repair, all have running water, and most have tended gardens. The houses date back some fifty years or more and their appearance reflects their age. It is not uncommon to hear roosters crowing and see chickens scratching in one of the yards. It is probable that when the last retiree passes on that mill camp will be levelled as has been the case with almost every other plantation camp in Hawai'i. To tour mill camp is to catch a glimpse of a rapidly disappearing way of life on O'ahu.

A word must be written about the "Goodale" for which the main street of the Waialua community is named. William W. Goodale was the first manager of the new Castle & Cooke Waialua Agricultural Company plantation and served for twenty-five years after 1898. He was an excellent choice and was an innovative and experienced manager. Every plantation field hand in Hawai'i owed his thanks to Goodale for it was he who in 1920 first used mechanical derricks to load bundles of harvested cane onto the cars that hauled it to the mill. After Goodale, the arduous and sometimes dangerous work of *hapai ko* became a thing of the past. Under Goodale's management the Waialua plantation became the first in Hawai'i to install a hydroelectric plant having a generating frequency deliberately matched to that of the commercial power grid with sales of excess power in mind.

While driving Kaukonahua Road toward Wahiawa you may spot a tall brick chimney in the fields off to the left. This is all that is left of the original Halstead sugarmill built in 1875 and abandoned in 1899. Until 1996, when the last of the Waialua plantation's cane was harvested, the fields surrounding this artifact were planted in sugarcane on both sides of Kaukonahua Road, as far as the eye could see.

The Birth Stones of Kukaniloko located north of Wahiawa are one of two locations in Hawai'i where the wives of high-ranking chiefs came to give birth. An impressive ceremony involving drums, chants, and offering of gifts accompanied the births that were attended by high chiefs and *kahuna*. The child would be named and honored by having its cord cut and hidden away. The site continues to be preserved as a sacred monument.

It has been recorded that as late as 1797 Kamehameha I made arrangements to have the birth of the child that turned out to be his son and heir, Liholiho (Kamehameha II), take place at the Birth Stones, but the illness of Queen Keopuolani (1778-1823) frustrated his plans. That is the last recorded attempt by the *ali'i*

The Sacred Birth Stones of Kukaniloko. The stones are located in a grove that is a short walk from the convenient parking space off Highway 80 north of Wahiawa. *(W. H. Dorrance)*

to make use of the site. Those who stop to view this site may wish to double back to Wilikina Drive to visit the attractions at Schofield Barracks.

Schofield Barracks is an "open base" and at present, civilians are free to enter the reservation. The Tropic Lightning Museum is located here. An armored personnel carrier, a Sherman tank, and two artillery pieces are parked on the lawn in front of the museum.

Macomb Road, leading to the museum, is named for Maj. Gen. Montgomery M. Macomb (1847-1924) who served as a senior commander in Hawai'i from 1911 to 1914. He is remembered for the impact he had in designing and implementing O'ahu's land defenses prior to and during World War I. The strong role he played

The Tropic Lightning Museum located on the Schofield Barracks reservation at the corner of Macomb Road and Waianae Avenue. (W. H. Dorrance)

was such that another road was also named for him on the Fort Shafter reservation.

The nearby large barracks appeared in the movie *From Here To Eternity,* based on the prize-winning James Jones novel. The buildings were constructed in the early 1920s and house soldiers of the 25th Infantry Division.

This division was activated in 1941 from elements of the Hawaiian Division and its motto "Tropic Lightning" gave the museum its name. The division served with great distinction in the Southwest Pacific campaigns during World War II and in the Korean War, and included regiments of local recruits and inductees. The museum honors their service as well as presenting exhibits that illustrate the history of this famous Army Barracks.

WAHIAWA

This community of 20,000 possesses one of the richest histories of any O'ahu location. The area, including the town, Schofield

A view from the parade ground of one of the three-story barracks at Schofield Barracks. A view of this barracks appeared in the movie *From Here to Eternity* based on the James Jones award-winning novel. *(W. H. Dorrance)*

Barracks, Wheeler Field, and pineapple fields, was originally the ancient *moku* of Wai'anae, Waialua, and Ewa. In 1913, in recognition of the growth of population within the region, the boundaries of a new district of Wahiawa were created.

Wahiawa was heavily forested before Capt. James Cook first visited Hawai'i in 1778. Four *heiau,* now destroyed, testified to the relatively dense occupancy of the area by Native Hawaiians.

From about 1800 to 1830 harvesting of the sandalwood forest of Wahiawa for the China trade helped sustain the solvency of the kingdom. As a consequence of this, few sandalwood trees can be found in Wahiawa today. Eucalyptus trees abound in the newly forested regions. In 1825 Wahiawa supplied logs to be used in the construction of Kawaiahao Church in Honolulu.

While the region lay dormant during the rest of the nineteenth century, in 1872 an event occurred that had great significance for O'ahu and Wahiawa. Maj. Gen. John McAllister Schofield (1831-1906) and Lt. Col. Barton Stone Alexander (1821?-1878), Corps of Engineers, visited Hawai'i. It was publicly stated that the visit was a vacation. Their real purpose was to study the usefulness of the kingdom's harbors for commerce and how such harbors could be defended. Curiously, the records reveal little of their conclusions other than that Schofield stated that the United States should demand a Pearl Harbor concession in return for granting reciprocity in free trade.

By 1899 Hawaiʻi was a territory of the United States and some 1,320 acres in Wahiawa were set aside for homesteads. The region lacked water and few lots were taken. In that same year, by Presidential Order, 14,400 parched acres were turned over to the War Department for use by the Army. It was thought that the area could by used for rest and recuperation of soldiers returning from the Philippines.

In 1901 James Drummond Dole (1877-1958) became the thirteenth homesteader when he took possession of some twelve acres. He incorporated the Hawaiian Pineapple Company, Ltd. (HAPCO), added to his acreage by lease, and in 1903 produced the first of years of pineapple crops. That same year an Army board inspected the Army's 14,400 acres and declared them undesirable because of lack of water. As a result, development of the area by the Army was delayed and Fort Shafter became the first permanent Army reservation in Hawaiʻi.

By 1906 the O.R.& L. railroad company had built a branch to Wahiawa to haul Dole's growing pineapple harvests to the Honolulu docks. HAPCO had outgrown its small Wahiawa cannery and Dole built a large cannery in Honolulu by 1907. Trains and then, beginning in 1947 when the O.R.& L. shut down, trucks hauled the crops to Honolulu.

In 1907, seeing that the Army wasn't using its 14,400 acres in Wahiawa, the Territorial Governor requested that the land be returned to the Territory for use as homesteads. But in 1908 the Army began construction on the site. An O.R.& L. railroad spur into the site was completed in 1909.

Fresh water was a problem in the location. A stream carrying fresh mountain water ran through the area. In 1900 the Wahiawa Water Works company began building a dam to create a lake-reservoir to capture the water. The dam was completed in 1907 and the resulting lake named Wilson Lake in memory of water works manager A.A. Wilson. Waialua Sugar Company (formerly Waialua Agricultural Company, Ltd.), purchased billions of gallons of this water yearly for irrigation and the rest supplies the surrounding community.

In 1909 the Army Reservation was named Schofield Barracks in memory of Lt. General John M. Schofield who had done so much to establish the Army's presence on Oʻahu. General Schofield was awarded the Congressional Medal of Honor for service in the Civil

War, and served as Commanding General of the Army from 1888 to 1895. It was a fitting choice.

In recognition of the growing population, in 1913 the district of Wahiawa was created by taking land from the neighboring districts of Waialua, 'Ewa, and Wai'anae. It was the first creation of a new O'ahu district in over five hundred years. The district was enlarged with land from the Wai'anae and 'Ewa districts in 1932.

In 1921 the Army's 4th Observation Squadron was moved from Luke Field (on Ford Island) to Schofield Barracks. In 1922 the former cavalry drill grounds in the southern part of the Schofield Reservation were set aside as the home for the squadron and called the Hawai'i Division Air Service Flying Field. In 1922 the field was renamed Wheeler Field in memory of Maj. Sheldon H. Wheeler (unk.-1921) who was killed in a crash at Luke Field in 1921.

In 1922 James Dole sold one-third of HAPCO to Castle & Cooke to raise money for expansion, and to buy the island of Lana'i. By 1932 Castle & Cooke controlled HAPCO and Dole was serving as a figurehead chairman of the board. Today HAPCO is part of Dole Food Company and his name lives on.

The December 7, 1941 Japanese attack had deadly consequences for the aircraft and personnel stationed at Wheeler Field. Thirty-seven Americans were killed and eighty-three of 153 aircraft based at Wheeler were destroyed or seriously damaged. Despite the damage six pilots stationed at Wheeler were able to take off, and they shot down eleven of the attackers. Considering the surprise attack it was a remarkable accomplishment by the American pilots.

In 1989 Wheeler Air Force Base was returned to the Army after serving over forty years as an Air Force installation. The Air Force obtained the Fort Kamehameha reservation located adjacent to Hickam Air Force Base in exchange for Wheeler.

Today the town of Wahiawa is a bustling community of military families, shop keepers, and pineapple workers. Schofield Barracks is the home of the Army's 25th Infantry division. Jim Dole and General Schofield would be pleased with what grew in their names on sparsely-settled and parched land in central O'ahu.

When the United States entered World War II, every mile of O'ahu's coastline was to be defended and a regiment of 8-inch railway-mounted guns was to play a key role. These large cannons, eight in number, were kept on the Fort Kamehameha reservation near the entrance to Pearl Harbor until needed. The guns were to be hauled by an Army locomotive over the O.R.& L. tracks to prepared emplacements around the island when hostilities threatened. What follows is the story of this unusual Army defense.

O'AHU'S SECRET RAILROAD

One of the mysteries of twentieth century O'ahu history is the unnoticed coming and going of a U. S. Army railroad system. This railroad system existed after 1920 and by 1946 all evidence of it had disappeared. Little other than a few photographs of rolling stock survive.

At the turn of the century, the railroad was the world-wide king of surface transportation. O'ahu had its share of railroads. Benjamin Dillingham's 36-inch, narrow-gauge O.R.& L. ran from the docks at Honolulu along the western shore of the island, around Ka'ena Point, and along the North Shore to Kahuku. Eventually a branch was constructed from Honolulu to Wahiawa when the Dole Pineapple Company became a thriving operation.

Developments made during the Great War of 1914-1918 led to O'ahu's secret railroad system. When the United States entered the war in 1917 it brought to the struggle several large-caliber railroad-mounted cannon that were removed from its many harbor defense forts. At the end of this war these railroad guns were returned to the United States.

It was the responsibility of the Army's Coast Artillery Corps to defend Honolulu and the Navy's base at Pearl Harbor. A strategy was developed that emphasized static fortifications near Honolulu and Pearl Harbor (Forts Ruger, Armstrong, Shafter, Kamehameha, Weaver, and Barrette), augmented by a mobile army at a central redoubt (Schofield Barracks), and mobile, large-caliber cannons. O'ahu's secret railroad system was born of this strategy.

Why not construct railroad-gun emplacements around the island at strategic defense localities as far south as Kahana Bay? These were built in advance to receive railroad guns when and if the island came under attack. There was no need to alarm the populace by permanently emplacing large cannons around the island. The railroad cannons could stay in storage within military reservations of Forts Kamehameha and Shafter, and be brought out to the dispersed emplacements when the island was threatened.

O'ahu's secret railroad system came into existence in December 1921 when the Army organized the Hawaiian Railway Battalion at Fort Kamehameha. This battalion, in 1922 redesignated the Forty-First Artillery Battalion, expanded to regimental strength in 1924. It received a steam locomotive and eight railroad cars, each mounting a 12-inch mortar. As used by the troops, the mortar emplacements were inaccurate and the mortars were replaced with 8-inch rifled guns in 1934, and the number of off-reservation emplacements were increased to eight.

During the December 7, 1941 attack, the railroad guns were temporarily bottled up at Fort Kamehameha when a Japanese bomb severed the tracks on Hickam Field. The tracks were soon repaired and four of the guns were moved to the west coast at Brown's Camp and four were moved to Kawailoa on the North Shore near Hale'iwa, awaiting an invasion that never came.

The Army recognized that because the roadbed ran close to the coast it was highly vulnerable to bombardment from offshore. In passing from Barbers Point north, the tracks were never more than a few yards from the shore and something more secure was needed if railroad transport of guns, personnel, and materiel were to be used during an attack.

The Army planned to construct a length of railroad track to connect the Wahiawa branch with the North Shore at Pu'uiki west of Hale'iwa.

Army train of 8-inch railroad guns on parade at Schofield Barracks circa 1936. The railroad tracks were put down temporarily to accommodate this review for visiting congressmen. *(U. S. Army Museum of Hawaii)*

This roadbed was to be constructed by Army personnel with great secrecy, . When completed it would be possible for Army trains to move from Honolulu to the North Shore through the center of the island and exposure to shell fire from offshore would be minimized. There is doubt that this roadbed was ever completed.

Little evidence of this secret Army railroad system remains. The tsunami of April 1946 wiped out much of the O.R.& L. roadbed and the railroad shut down soon afterwards. Tracks were uprooted over much of the O.R.& L. and scrapped. A length of track runs through the northern edge of the old Fort Kamehameha reservation, and a few old Army flat cars are preserved and used by the Hawaiian Railway Society located in Ewa.

The story of what the native Hawaiians knew as Moku ʻUmeʻume is the story of Ford Island.

MOKU ʻUMEʻUME

This is a small island located in the middle of the Pearl Harbor lagoon. It is entirely surrounded by water deep enough to accommodate oceangoing vessels. The island measures about 1-1/2 mile long by 3/4 mile wide in a roughly elliptical shape. Almost everybody knows it as "Ford Island".

Moku ʻUmeʻume means "Island of the game ʻUme ʻUme." The natives indulged in this game in centuries past. It began with a gathering of commoners and chiefs around a bonfire on the island. As evening fell the leader chanted a lascivious song. Couples formed a ring about the leader and the fire. As he chanted, the leader used a coconut frond as a wand to touch a woman and then a man. The couple then retired to spend the night together. While they might very well be married, they weren't married to their partners that night. It was a game of short-term mate swapping. At daylight all returned to their respective mates and that game was over.

The influential Spaniard, Francisco de Paula Marin, took possession of the island around 1810. He raised sheep, hogs, goats, and rabbits to supply his profitable shipprovisioning business. During this period it was called Marin's Island.

Following a turbulent era of unsettled land ownership in the then-young kingdom, ownership of the island passed to a trust formed for the son of a prominent Honolulu physician, Dr. Seth Porter Ford (1818-1866). Thus was established the basis for the modern day name for Moku 'Ume'ume. The son, Seth Porter Ford, Jr., took possession of the island about 1885.

In 1891 Ford sold the island to the the John I'i estate. This estate had vast landholdings in and around Pearl Harbor. Judge John Papa I'i (1800?-1870) was a Native Hawaiian of noble parentage who had served Kings Kamehameha II, III, and IV. Charles A. Brown married Judge I'i's daughter and heir, and managed the estate from 1887 to 1916, at which time his son George I'i Brown took over.

This family is well-known to dedicated Hawai'i golfers. Another of Charles A. Brown's sons, Francis I'i Brown, was a champion amateur golfer in the islands in the years before World War II. The magnificent golf course at Mauna Lani on the Big Island of Hawai'i is named for Francis I'i Brown, who gave generously of his time and resources to support the sport.

In 1899 the Oahu Sugar Company leased Ford Island from the I'i estate. Some 300-odd acres of sugar cane were planted, and dockage was constructed on the island and on Waipi'o Peninsula to facilitate transfer of cane harvests by barge on the way to the mill at Waipahu.

With the coming of World War I, the War Department was concerned about the defenses of the large and growing U.S. Navy establishment at Pearl Harbor. Ford Island was selected as a site for placing land-based guns to defend the harbor.

In 1916 two small parcels of Ford Island were acquired from the I'i estate by the War Department. These sites were selected for two two-gun batteries of casemated, 6-inch rifled guns. The locations were at the southwest and northeast corners of the island. They were completed in 1917 and named Batteries Boyd and Henry Adair served on until 1925 when they were inactivated and the guns removed. A recent search of Ford Island revealed that the structures survive.

In the fall of 1916 the War Department sent Capt. John F. Curry to O'ahu to select a site for a squadron that he was to command. His initial complement of aircraft would be flying boats, so he looked for a watery location and recommended Ford Island.

In 1917 the War Department purchased the island and the Oahu Sugar Company surrendered its leasehold. It was understood by the

War Department that both the Army and the Navy could make use of Ford Island. The initial contingent of Army personnel arrived in

Northwest tip of Ford Island showing the casemates of the long-disarmed Battery Adair. Two 6-inch rifles were emplaced within the casemates intended for land defense of Pearl Harbor. The guns were removed in 1925 and the battery structure was incorporated into the foundation of a flag officer's residence. *(U. S. Army Museum of Hawaii)*

September 1918. These troops established the first independent Army Air Service station in Hawai'i.

In 1919 the new station was officially designated "Luke Field," named for World War I ace Frank Luke, killed in action over the Western front. Pursuit planes and bombers were soon delivered by ship. Luke Field grew to become a sizeable base. It was noted for its gymnasium, post exchange, and the convenience of the on-base facilities. The field was pleasant duty for the Army's airmen. The friendly surroundings of Honolulu were nearby and accessible by ferry boat.

By late 1935 it was apparent that the island was becoming too crowded for joint Army and Navy operations. A deal was struck. The Army would take possession of the Navy's field near Sunnyvale, California, in return for giving up North Island in San Diego and Ford Island to the Navy. At the same time the Army purchased land to construct a new air base that became Hickam Field.

In 1937 the move of the Army's contingent across the bay to Hickam began in earnest, and the Navy took exclusive possession of the island. Its air station figured heavily in the Japanese attack of December 7, 1941. Of the seventy-eight aircraft on the ground when the attack hit Ford Island, thirty-three were destroyed. World War II was the busiest time for Ford Island. The runway grew until it covered the entire center of the island. Hangars and auxiliary buildings filled almost all available space.

When you visit the west side of the island you encounter a little-known military memorial. It is the remains of the sunken battleship

Utah located about fifty yards offshore. The *Utah* was obsolete and used as a target ship by the time of the December 7, 1941 attack.

Damage on the ramp at Ford Island after the December 7, 1941 Japanese attack. *(U. S. Navy)*

Nevertheless, from the air she resembled an active battle wagon so was bombed and sunk. *Utah* was one of the first vessels to be attacked and she rolled on her side and sank, trapping much of her crew below decks with considerable loss of life. The bodies of fifty-eight crew members are entombed within the hulk of *Utah*.

The well-tended residences near the *Utah* memorial date from the 1920s and were erected by the Army to house the families of officers assigned to Luke Field, the Army air base then located on Ford Island. They are an excellent example of quartermasters' architecture of that era.

With the advent of earth satellites and improvements in range and speed of modern aircraft after the war, a large Navy air station near Pearl Harbor no longer made strategic sense. In 1962 the Navy officially inactivated Ford Island as an air base. Today the old structures

Sunken target ship *Utah* entombing the bodies of fifty-eight crew members. *(W. H. Dorrance)*

serve as Naval housing, and some of the buildings are headquarters for a few operational commands. Until recently, a tour of the island left you with the feeling of having visited a vast military ruin. However, this is changing. In 1994 the Navy announced that the island will be used for newly-constructed housing for Navy personnel and that a causeway-bridge will replace the ferry to the island. This construction was recently completed (1998) and soon the island will begin a new episode in its history.

Large cranes used to unload Matson and SeaLand container ships stand out and mark the shoreline of Sand Island. The section of the city that you look over when viewing Sand Island is Iwilei. Its story adds spice to the history of O'ahu.

IWILEI

Lusty Iwilei, an industrial section of Honolulu, lies adjacent to the dock area. At first blush there is little that draws more than passing interest. It is only when you dig into Iwilei's past that an interesting story emerges.

With the rediscovery of these islands by Captain Cook, Hawai'i's reputation for *aloha* and hospitality began to spread around the world. In no small measure this was due to the behavior of some of the native women.

Ships visiting soon after Cook were met by schools of native women who swam out to greet them. More often than not these cheerful women would spend the evenings and nights aboard ship in the company of sailors starved for female companionship. Initially no payment was asked.

Soon, however, the native women grew canny. Their fathers or mates knew that the visitors had useful items to trade for the ladies' favors. Iron nails, sailcloth, knives, and daggers became staples in what became a trade. Further, the women no longer swam to the ships. Their attraction drew the sailors ashore and this kind of *aloha* became a commercial enterprise.

Honolulu became a favorite reprovisioning stop for the increasing number of vessels plying the Pacific. Unfortunately for the natives it was not all a blessing. The visitors brought with them previously unknown venereal diseases and pestilences. The native population began to die off as a result.

By 1860 the situation called for drastic measures. The legislature created the Act that was intended to mitigate the situation. It read in part:

"Whereas, the evils and diseases arising from prostitution are widespread and apparent, carrying death to thousands of the Hawaiian race, and preventing the increase of the population; and it being impossible to suppress and crush out prostitution but that its evils and diseases may be combatted, circumscribed and diminished...

"Therefore, be it enacted by the King...that a system of regulation of prostitution be established including the registration of prostitutes, regular medical examination of them...and treatment of infected prostitutes by the health department free of charge."

King Kamehameha IV signed off on the Act which then became law. This Act described the thinking regarding prostitution up to and into World War II. Providing a prostitute registered as such and passed regular examinations, she was free to ply her trade.

While prostitution was condoned, the city's elders felt it had to be somehow contained. What was needed was a "red light district" within which commercial *aloha* could be dispensed, and to which participants were to be constrained.

Iwilei was a natural location for this resort. The terminal of the O.R.& L. railroad was located there. Nearby on the shore were the docks for inter-island steamships. Then, of course, the enterprise was decently out of sight of the central business district, yet only a few blocks away.

Sometime before 1900 a "stockade" with five entrances was established in Iwilei. Police rules were posted near the entrance and a policeman patrolled to control unruly clients.

As time went on, the enterprising madams of Iwilei expanded their reservation until it covered several blocks. The district acquired the dubious reputation of a world-class bordello. Honolulu began to be compared with such wide-open and exotic ports as Port Said, Marseilles, Port au Prince, and the Yoshiwara district in Japan.

Writers like Somerset Maugham wrote vaguely titillating stories based on the stockade at Iwilei. It was a curious development for a city whose legitimate commerce was under the ironclad rule of the descendents of missionaries. Something had to be done.

In 1905 the legislature repealed the governing Act. Committees were formed to study the situation. In the meantime nature took its course, and the trade continued to flourish under the old rules.

Honolulu was a growing city of almost 40,000 residents. While the city enjoyed most modern developments, it lacked a gas

Street scene interior to Iwilei stockade circa 1912. *(R. J. Baker Collection, Bishop Museum)*

distribution company. William Richards Castle, William Waterhouse Dimond, and Albert N. Campbell obtained a gas distribution franchise in 1904. Hawai'i being a U.S. Territory at the time, the franchise was created by an act in Washington and signed off by President Theodore Roosevelt. Their company manufactured pipeline gas using a process that liberated the gas contained within crude oil.

It was a dirty process so the gasworks was located in Iwilei, removed from the central business district and residential areas. As a consequence no fewer than 180 "ladies of the evening" were displaced. They simply moved over and became neighbors of the gasworks.

One night in November 1916 the police swooped down on the stockade and closed it off. The girls were rounded up, arrested, given suspended sentences of one year, and ordered to desist from their amorous pusuits.

That order was obeyed just as other such orders are obeyed. The stockade was closed to prostitution forever, however. Prostitution in Iwilei was no more and the gasworks had lost its colorful neighbors.

In 1901 James Dole's Hawaiian Pineapple Company, Ltd. had started its pineapple plantation on the central plains of O'ahu. By 1907 it had outgrown its field cannery so a new operation was built in Iwilei. The Dole cannery was soon joined by others in the same community.

In 1927 the Dole company built a unique curiosity to amuse the casual observer. To all intents it appeared to be a giant pineapple. Sixty-two feet high and over 100 feet in circumference it towered above the cannery building. It was a camouflaged emergency water supply of 100,000 gallons backing up a sprinkler system protecting the 1,500,000 square foot factory complex. For over sixty years it captured the eyes of visitors to Honolulu until removed in 1993. The building was replaced by today's Cannery Square shopping center as Iwilei's premier attraction.

Recognition grew among preservationists that the "Dole Pineapple" was an important artifact that always stood out in the memories of visitors to the islands, and that it should somehow be

"Dole Pineapple." Dismantled in 1993, a preservationist group is currently working for its restoration. *(W. H. Dorrance)*

restored. Fortunately, the pineapple had been carefully disassembled when removed and the pieces retained. The Historic Hawai'i Foundation has formed a task force dedicated to raising funds for restoration of this venerable Honolulu landmark. Soon visitors driving into the city from the airport will again be able to "spot the pineapple."

There is little that is left of the interesting past in today's Iwilei. Even the enterprises that displaced the stockade are yielding to progress. By September 1974 a modern synthetic natural gas plant was operating near Barbers Point, and the Iwilei plant shut down and was placed on a standby basis. In 1987 the reliability of the new plant was considered proven and demolition of the old Iwilei plant began. Nothing remains of this old neighbor of Honolulu's "ladies of the night."

DOWNTOWN HONOLULU

Until the turn of the nineteenth-century, the Native Hawaiians knew this place as "Kou" (as in *kou* tree). Visits by foreign ships greatly increased during King Kamehameha I's reign and in the vernacular the name became "Honolulu" (protected harbor). For over a century afterwards it was the only deep and sheltered harbor in the kingdom.

Because of the increasing commerce brought by ships, in 1807 Kamehameha I moved his residence from Waikiki to Honolulu. Then in 1817 he ordered the expatriate Englishman John Young to oversee construction of a substantial fort at Honolulu's shore to control and protect the anchorage. With the growing importance of the fort's surroundings, after 1832 the governor of Oahu, High Chief Mataio Kekuana'oa (1794-1868), father of the princes who later became Kings Kamehameha IV and Kamehameha V, resided in the fort until 1849. It wasn't until 1857 that the two-story and 40-cannon fort was levelled to make room for warehouses. Today's Fort Street Mall and Fort Street point the way to the former location of the fort.

Numerous buildings survive in downtown Honolulu that owe their existence to long-gone commercial activity and the community's sense of historical preservation. Within a walk of seven blocks east and west, and three blocks north and south you can inspect many historical sites and buildings that grace downtown Honolulu. A good time to explore the area is Sunday morning or afternoon when traffic is minimal. Making the walk will take you through one of the cleanest, most beautiful and well-maintained big city locales in the United States.

Start at the corner of Bethel Street and Merchant Street with the intention of walking toward Diamond Head. This corner is close to the location to which Kamehameha I moved from Waikiki. At that time Merchant Street was a dusty and unnamed trail. The houses of high chiefs lined the ocean-side and an open field devoted to drills and games was located on the inland-side of the trail. By 1850, however, the chief's residences had been replaced by fledgling business enterprises and a two-story, coral government building. Soon after, the narrow street was officially named "Merchant Street."

Second-generation structures began to be built after the King Kamehameha V Post Office, completed in 1871, was located on the northeast corner of Bethel and Merchant Streets. Still standing, it is the oldest reinforced concrete building in the United States, as officially proclaimed by the American Society of Civil Engineers. Small windows are visible through which clerks interacted with customers, and one can imagine lines of people under the open-air portico awaiting service. The building served as downtown Honolulu's post office until a new facility was opened in 1922.

Across Merchant Street, and opposite the park on the Diamond Head-side of the post office, is the original Bishop Bank Building that is now a law office. Charles R. Bishop and partner William A. Aldrich (1824-1892} founded the enterprise 1858 that eventually became Bishop Bank (now First Hawaiian Bank). The elegant two-story building was completed in 1878 and was occupied by the bank until 1923. For decades during the early years the growing sugar industry owed much to the Bishop Bank's support. Along with the post office it survived the disastrous 1886 Chinatown fire.

Bishop had earlier distinguished himself when, in 1850, he married Princess Bernice Pauahi. After she died in 1884, he established Bernice P. Bishop Museum in her memory and established a trust to perpetuate its existence. Princess Pauahi was the last of the Kamehameha line of chiefs.

Continue toward Diamond Head down Merchant Street to the next intersection with Fort Street. The Judd Building (now the First Federal Building) is located on the southeast corner. Designed by Oliver G. Traphagen and completed in 1899, it was named for the family patriarch Dr. Gerrit P. Judd who first arrived in Hawaii in 1828. It was the tallest building constructed in Honolulu.

That claim didn't last long. The six-story Stangenwald Building was completed next door in 1901. It was designed by the prominent *kama'aina* architect Charles W. Dickey (1871-1942) and still serves as well-located office space. Before recent modifications the open foyer extended to the roof and every level had a balcony. The building housed the headquarters of Alexander & Baldwin company for twenty-five years until the Alexander & Baldwin building was completed. A visit reveals a spacious foyer, and space for enterprises in the basement, that suggests how it was in the beginning. It's a charming old building.

Hugo Stangenwald (1829-1899) was a German medical man who arrived in Hawaii to stay in 1851. Long known to the Native Hawaiians as "the instantaneous healer." it was his misfortune to die before the structure named for him was completed.

Turn right onto Bishop Street at the next corner and you will see the steps and facade of the handsome Alexander & Baldwin Building. It was completed in 1929 and is one of two surviving buildings constructed in that era by members of the "Big Five" sugar oligarchy (Alexander & Baldwin, Castle & Cooke, C. Brewer & Co., Theo H. Davies & Co., and American Factors). The former C. Brewer headquarters, completed in 1930 at the northeast corner of Fort and Queen Streets, is the other survivor. The prominent architect Charles Dickey designed the striking Alexander & Baldwin Building.

It is dedicated to the memories of company founders Samuel Thomas Alexander and Henry Perrine Baldwin, both sons of missionaries. Alexander was born at Waioli, Kaua'i and Baldwin at Lahaina, Maui where their parents maintained missions for the Congregational Church.

Missionary descendant Francis S. Morgan told how the design of this building happened to depart from the appearance of the now-gone Theo H. Davies Building built across Bishop Street a few years before. It was part of the lore passed along to him during his forty-years as a Theo H. Davies executive. It seems that in 1918 every member of the Big Five was contemplating building a new headquarters and were close neighbors in downtown Honolulu. Being public-spirited they got together and decided that they could improve the city's appearance if they agreed on new buildings with compatible architecture.

The Theo H. Davies company first constructed a utilitarian, four-story building at the northeast corner of Bishop and Queen Streets (replaced in 1970 with the Davies Pacific Center). While its attractions included an interior courtyard, the exterior resembled somber and dark coral stone. This didn't appeal to the remaining four of the Big Five, so they broke the informal agreement and two of them employed Dickey to produce buildings that they deemed to be more suitable to semi-tropical Honolulu.

Aloha Tower. For years after its completion in 1926, the Aloha Tower dominated the Honolulu waterfront and was the tallest structure in Honolulu. *(W.H. Dorrance)*

Further along Bishop Street toward the harbor, you will see the Aloha Tower in the distance. The ten-story structure was completed in 1926 and was the first to surpass the height of the Stangenwald Building. When renovations have been completed, you will be able to take an elevator to an observation deck at the top of the tower for a view of Honolulu Harbor. The surrounding Aloha Tower Marketplace is an excellent spot to pause for lunch while watching traffic in the harbor.

The Hawaii Maritime Center is located on Pier 7, Diamond Head of the marketplace. This fine museum contains exhibits that do much to explain the development of modern-day Honolulu and the island kingdom in general. A four-masted and square-rigged sailing vessel, *Falls of Clyde,* is berthed next to the Center and can be inspected. This rare example of large commercial sailing ships was built in Scotland in 1878 and served into the twentieth century before being laid-up as an oil barge. She was owned by the Matson Company between 1898 and 1906 when she transported freight and passengers on the San Francisco-Hawaii run. Her restoration continues and much is owed to a host of tireless volunteers.

Return inland on Bishop Street. The Dillingham Transportation Building is on the northeast corner of Nimitz Boulevard and Bishop Street. This Italianate structure is a memorial to Oahu railroad tycoon Benjamin F. Dillingham and dates back to 1928. Walk through one of the two arcades off Bishop Street for a view of a nicely-landscaped courtyard, one of several that grace downtown Honolulu. In those by-gone days every businessman knew, or thought he knew, every other businessman in town.

Curiously, Dillingham's O.R.& L. railroad never got any closer to this building than its terminal, still there at the corner of Iwilei Street and N. King Street some ten blocks west in Iwilei.

Continuing inland, turn right when you reach King Street. If you were walking this tour before 1972 you would have seen the magnificent Alexander Young Hotel where Pauahi Tower and Tamarind Park are located. For seventy years this six-story and block-long building was Honolulu's preeminent hotel. It was here that outer-island sugar men would stay when they visited Honolulu to transact business with the Hawaiian Sugar Planters' Association and members of the Big Five.

Alexander Young (1832-1910), from Scotland, arrived in Hilo in 1865 where he established a machine shop and foundry. His holdings grew to include interests in Big Island sugar plantations, a stake in Theo H. Davies & Co., and an interest in the Moana Hotel along with ownership of the Alexander Young hotel.

Leaving this site haunted by now-gone capitalists, walk three blocks Diamond Head down King Street to the entrance to the Iolani Palace grounds. The palace is the only such vestige of a monarchy within the United States.

King Kalakaua ordered it constructed to replace the termite-ridden and smaller edifice that served as a palace on the site from 1845 to 1878. Iolani Palace was completed in 1882. King Kalakaua was filled with visions of the pomp and circumstance accorded royalty when he returned from his precedent-making world tour in 1880. So it was that he called for an official coronation ceremony for him and his consort, Queen Kap'iolani, in February 1883. The ceremony also served as a grand opening of the new palace.

Aliiolani Hale is located across King Street from the palace grounds, and a celebrated statue of King Kamehameha I stands in front of the building. A visit to the interior of Aliiolani Hale is time well spent. An easily-accessible diorama and movie describe the development of a legal system in Hawaii starting with ancient times and moving into the present. The State's Supreme Court chambers and courtroom are located inside.

Moving further Diamond Head on King Street, you pass the imposing Hawaii State Library building on the left, next to the palace

Iolani Palace was constructed in 1882. The present band stand was originally located close to and in front of the palace to be used in the 1883 coronation ceremonies. *(W.H. Dorrance)*

grounds. This building was completed in 1913 using funds contributed by the prominent mainland philanthropist Andrew Carnegie (1835-1919). The building has been greatly enlarged but the original entrance foyer and facade remain. This is one of a very few Carnegie libraries that is still standing and used for its intended purposes. Carnegie funded over one thousand libraries throughout the United States and its territories.

Kawaiahao (fresh water pool of Hao, a chief or chiefess) Church is located diagonally across from the State Library at the intersection

The Hawaii State Library, first completed in 1913. This fine library houses the headquarters of the Hawai'i State Library system and contains a vast collection of Hawai'i and Pacific volumes. *(W.H. Dorrance)*

of King and Punchbowl Streets. This coral-stone church was constructed between 1837 and 1842 as a public works project directed by King Kamehameha III. Coral stones were cut from offshore reefs and laboriously hauled to the church site by Native Hawaiian volunteers. Rev. Hiram Bingham (1789-1869), who arrived in Hawaii in 1820 with the first company of American missionaries, designed the building and served as its first pastor.

A story is told how a Wilkes Expedition member visiting Oahu in 1840, one John Dale, attended Sunday services in then-incomplete Kawaiahaʻo Church accompanied by King Kamehameha III. "When will the church be finished?" the visitor asked. The king replied, "The church will be finished when it IS finished." Thus was ended the interrogation.

Across Kawaiahao Street from the church is the Hawaiian Mission Children's Society compound (membership limited to *kamaʻaina* descendants of the missionaries). For decades it served as the headquarters of the American Congregationalist Sandwich Islands Mission, and the buildings are the three oldest Western structures in the islands. The two-story, white frame house was completed in 1821 with pre-cut timbers shipped from Boston on the ship *Tartar*. This is the oldest wooden house in Hawaii and was used as a rectory for the church, being occupied for a time by, among others, Rev. Bingham. The large coral house, completed in 1831, was initially used as a the residence of the Levi Chamberlain family. The small coral house, constructed in 1841, was used as a printing office and storehouse. The fourth structure on the compound serves as the office, library, and archives of the Hawaiian Historical Society.

The visit to the mission house compound completes your Central Oahu tour. Now you can look forward to West Oʻahu.

PART THREE

WEST O'AHU TOUR

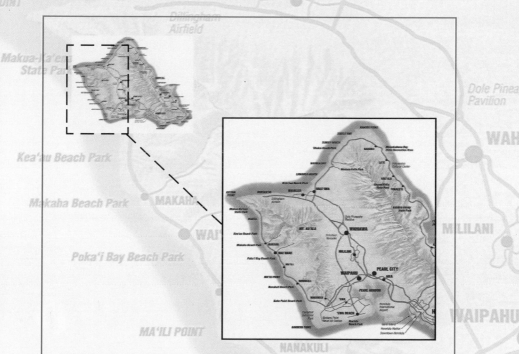

Driving time: Eight hours depending on stops made along the way.

TheBus time: At least a day depending on stops made along, the way.

INTRODUCTION TO WEST O'AHU

THIS DESCRIPTION IS made difficult by the wandering and seemingly perverse directions taken by West O'ahu's streets. The main streets, other than the freeways and highways, are often over one-hundred years old and in the beginning were rutted and unpaved paths that skirted the contours of the many hillocks, hills, and mountain ridges. These paths were eventually paved and now serve as the streets and roads of residential and rural O'ahu. As a consequence, street maps are often confusing and the tour of West O'ahu is difficult to describe without burdening the reader with detail. Nevertheless, the most direct routes between attractions are described.

Your first stop will be the Arizona Memorial. We will assume your tour starts in Waikiki, but you can join the tour anywhere along the way. Leaving Waikiki Beach, take Ala Wai Boulevard to McCully Street, McCully Street to Dole Street, Dole Street to Alexander Street, then to Highway H-1 westbound. Four miles down the freeway take the right fork to continue on the airport-bound elevated Highway H-1. This is a tricky access so prepare for it by driving in the right-hand lane. Some 2-3/4 miles along elevated H-1 take the well-marked off-ramp to Highway 99, Kamehameha Highway, leading to the entrance to Arizona Memorial. Drive 1-1/3 mile after entering the highway and turn left onto Arizona Memorial Drive. Park in the lot to the right. Parking is free and it is a short walk to the Memorial and to the adjacent, privately-run, Submarine Museum.

Your next stop on the West O'ahu Tour is Hawaii's Plantation Village located within the Waipahu Cultural Garden Park. Getting to the village from the Arizona Memorial can be a challenge given the irregular layout of the streets in West O'ahu, so we will make use of a little local knowledge.

Turn left onto Highway 99, Kamehameha Highway, when leaving the memorial park. Get into the right-hand lane. After almost 1/3 mile turn right onto road marked "Stadium." Soon after, take right fork marked "Honolulu." Get into left-hand lane and after about 1/2 mile turn left onto Kahuapaani Street. Proceed almost a mile down Kahuapaani and turn right at sign marked H-1 WEST PEARL CITY to circle back and enter Highway H-1 going west.

A little over 4-1/2 miles after entering Highway H-1 you will encounter the clearly marked "Waipahu, Exit 8B," on the right. Take this exit that leads to Farrington Highway, Highway 90. Continue two miles down Farrington Highway and turn right onto Waipahu Depot Street. After about 1/10 mile (at the sugarmill) turn left onto Waipahu Street, and a little over 1/4 mile down Waipahu Street you encounter the entrance to the Waipahu Cultural Center on the left. Turn left and you arrive at the parking lot for Hawaii's Plantation Village. Parking is free.

Your next stop on the West O'ahu Tour takes you to the railroad yard of the Hawaiian Railway Society. Turn left onto Waipahu Street when leaving the cultural park and proceed about one mile to Leoku Street. (There is no stoplight, and a blue sign on corner reads "POLICE.") Turn left here and drive about 1/5 mile to Farrington Highway where you turn right and get into the left-hand lane. Drive about 1/2 mile further, going under the bridge, and turn left at sign marked "76 SOUTH EWA BEACH" to enter Fort Weaver Road. Drive two miles to Renton Road and turn right. The Hawaiian Railway Society is located a little over 1-1/2 miles further at the end of Renton Road, close to the Barbers Point Naval Air Station fence. To reach the yard you will pass through the restored Ewa Plantation Company mill camp residences.

To reach Fort Barrette from the Hawaiian Railway Society yard, retrace your drive back to Fort Weaver Road and turn left. After 1-3/4 mile you arrive at the intersection with Highway H-1. Enter Highway H-1 going west or Wai'anae-bound. After 3-

1/2 miles take the Fort Barrette Road and Barbers Point NAS exit and turn left toward the ocean. Fort Barrette is located on the hillock known as Pu'u Kapolei about 1/2 mile down the road on the right-hand side. You can park along the road to get a better view of some of the fort's installations if you haven't made arrangements with the city's Ewa Complex Manager's office to get behind the fence.

To drive to Wai'anae, return to Highway H-1 on Fort Barrette Road and enter the highway going west toward Wai'anae. Within the next mile the highway becomes Farrington Highway and about eleven miles beyond that point, after enjoying scenes of the beaches to the left, you will enter the community of Wai'anae.

It is possible to proceed another eight miles north of Wai'anae to Yokohama Bay, located about 2-3/4 miles short of Ka'ena Point. The land is sparsely settled but the fishing offshore is rewarding, and it is believed that the bay was named by the many Japanese fishermen who fish there. Makua Valley, on the inland side of the road, has been used as a military training area since World War II. It is forbidden to drive north beyond Yokohama Beach to Ka'ena Point.

This completes your tour of West O'ahu. Your return to Honolulu and Waikiki Beach is straightforward. Just retrace your route down Farrington Highway to Highway H-1. Enter Highway H-1 and follow the Honolulu signs all the way. Take the Nimitz off-ramp after passing the airport. Follow Nimitz to Ala Moana, and Ala Moana to Kalakaua and you are home again. Your drive covered 96 miles, including all side trips.

DIRECTIONS FOR TAKING THEBUS

Plan on doing the entire tour in two segments, each taking at least half a day.

The first takes you to the Arizona Memorial, Hawai'i's Plantation Village, and the Hawaiian Railway Society railroad yard before returning you to Ala Moana Center and Waikiki Beach. This segment takes the better part of a day's daylight hours. The second segment is equally time-consuming and takes you past the Arizona Memorial, to Fort Barrette, up the west coast to beyond Wai'anae, returning to Ala Moana Center.

Use bus nos. 8, 19, 20, 47, or 58, running on Kuhio Avenue to get from Waikiki Beach to Ala Moana. Transfer to bus no. 47 at Ala Moana Shopping Center. Bus no. 47 stops at the Arizona Memorial before moving on to Waipahu and Kapolei.

After visiting the memorial, reboard bus no. 47 bound for Waikele-Kapolei at Arizona Memorial. The bus will take you down Waipahu Street to the entrance to Hawaii's Plantation Village. Exit the bus there to visit the village.

Those visiting the railroad yards using TheBus should reboard no. 47 bound for Waikele-Kapolei at the cultural park. Exit no. 47 at the stop on Leoole Street, walk cross Leoole Street and go around the corner to the bus stop on Farrington Highway. Transfer to bus no. 48 bound for Ewa Mill. Exit the bus at the end of Renton Road opposite the railroad yard. After visiting the yard, reboard bus no. 48 to return to Ala Moana Center.

Those visiting Fort Barrette should transfer to bus no. 50 in Waipahu and take it to Kapolei. The visit to Fort Barrette will require about a mile walk from the nearest bus stop. Return to the Waipahu boarding stop by reboarding bus no. 50 bound for Honolulu.

Complete the West O'ahu by exiting bus no. 50 in Waipahu and transfer to Wai'anae-bound bus no. 51 that will take you beyond Wai'anae to Makaha Beach, and return you to Ala Moana Center.

Remember that fare payment is required each time you reboard TheBus so come armed with enough dollar bills, one for each stop you plan to make. The bus drivers do not make change.

CHAPTER ELEVEN

WAIKIKI TO 'EWA

Arizona MEMORIAL

IS THERE AN adult American who doesn't understand that the event precipitating the entrance of the United States into World War II took place right here on O'ahu?

It was the Japanese Imperial Navy's aerial attack on the morning of December 7, 1941 that drew the U.S. into the war. The attack is remembered as a monumental defeat for U.S. forces and the Arizona Memorial is dedicated to the memory of some 2,600 Americans who lost their lives during the treacherous attack. Over 1,100 of those Americans are entombed on the sunken battleship *Arizona*.

In the early morning hours of Sunday, December 7, 1941 an Imperial Japanese Navy task force arrived at a location about 220 miles due north of O'ahu. Six Japanese aircraft carriers made up the heart of the striking force. An attack was launched in two waves. The first, consisting of forty-nine high-level bombers, forty torpedo bombers, fifty-one dive bombers, and forty-three fighters, was launched at about 6:00 a.m. and arrived over Pearl Harbor shortly before 8:00 a.m. The second wave, consisting of fifty-four high-level bombers, eighty dive bombers, and thirty-six fighters, was launched about 7:15 a.m. and arrived at Pearl Harbor about 9:00 a.m. The mission called for high-level and torpedo bombers in the first wave and the dive bombers in the second wave to attack the vessels in Pearl Harbor. The rest of the bombers and some of the fighters were to attack the various air fields in an effort to catch and destroy defending aircraft on the ground.

The mission was highly successful from the Japanese perspective. The heart of the U.S. Navy Pacific Fleet was crippled as four of eight battleships in the harbor were sunk and the other four heavily damaged. Three light cruisers and three destroyers also were sunk or damaged. The target ship *Utah* was sunk beyond salvage. The total Army, Navy, Marine and civilian deaths exceeded 2,600 and the wounded overwhelmed O'ahu's medical facilities for weeks on end.

Nor was that all. The Japanese had feared that their approach to the island would be discovered before their bombers did their work. The hundreds of American fighter aircraft known to be on the island could rise to meet the attack. Their fears were in vain. The attack was a complete surprise and their fighters caught Marine, Navy, and Army aircraft defenders at Ewa Station, Ford Island and Kane'ohe Bay Naval Stations, Bellows, Wheeler, and Hale'iwa Army fields, all off guard. They were able to strafe the grounded aircraft with near impunity. One hundred and eighty-eight U.S. aircraft were destroyed and 159 were seriously damaged. The Japanese withdrew with loss of a mere 29 aircraft. By any measure it was an enormous victory for the Imperial Japanese Navy.

It gave the Japanese a temporary advantage soon to be overwhelmed by aroused American will and might. The attack had missed the two American aircraft carriers that fortuitously were at sea on maneuvers, and unaccountably left the exposed Navy fuel tanks on the Pearl Harbor Reservation untouched. These events conspired to contribute to the Japanese defeat when they attempted to seize Midway Island the first week in June 1942. Four large Japanese carriers were sunk in that battle and the Imperial Japanese Fleet was weakened to an extent from which it never recovered. The tides of war then turned in favor of the United States.

The superstructure of the U.S.S. *Arizona* capsizing after Japanese bombs caused explosion and subsequent sinking while entombing some 1,100 crew members. *(Natiional Archives)*

"Remember Pearl Harbor!" That was the rallying cry in the wake of the attack as America's industrial might rose to the occasion. And when the war was won in 1945 the attack that began the hostilities for the United States did not go unremembered. There were over 1,100 Americans entombed in the sunken *Arizona*. Their sacrifice, and the sacrifices of 1,500 others was not about to be forgotten. Private funds were solicited and an architect commissioned to design and build an appropriate memorial with the sunken vessel as the centerpiece.

The memorial is staffed by the National Park Service and consists of a complex on shore opposite Ford Island, and the memorial structure erected over the sunken *Arizona* at the Ford Island anchorage. The shore complex includes a theater and gift shop stocked with memorabilia. A visit, at no cost, consists of a twenty-minute documentary film shown in the theater followed by a round trip by launch to visit the *Arizona*. The tours are conducted in groups and each takes two hours. Unless you are in the first 7:30 a.m. group, you can expect a wait of as much as two or three hours before your group is called.

It is a curious fact that the architect who won the competition to design the U.S.S. Arizona Memorial was Alfred Pries, Austrian-born. He was detained on December 8, 1941 and interned in a Sand Island camp as a suspected German National before his release, as innocent, in March 1942. He and his wife became U.S. citizens in 1946. Such are the strange twists and turns of fate.

Should your group visiting the memorial clearly require an hour or longer wait, use the time to visit the privately-run Submarine Museum located nearby. One of the attractions is a guided tour through the Submarine *Bowfin* that served long and successfully through World War II. The *Bowfin* began its war-time service by rescuing American officers in the Philippines who had escaped their Japanese captors following the collapse of the American defenses, and went on to include sinking several enemy vessels until the war ended. The exhibits in the nearby museum illustrate the history of U.S. Navy submarines in Hawaiian waters beginning with pre-World War I service.

You will drive through the former sugar town of 'Aiea when you leave the memorial, bound for Hawaii's Plantation Village in Waipahu.

'AIEA

'Aiea was known to the ancient Hawaiians as an *ahupua'a* within the *moku* of 'Ewa. Modern residents know 'Aiea as a bedroom community located north of the East Loch of Pearl Harbor. 'Aiea was one of twelve *ahupua'a* that had its southern boundary at the shore of Pearl Harbor. These comparatively small and narrow land divisions were heavily populated by natives because of the fishing rights at the many ponds lining the shore in the harbor lagoon. Mountain water was abundant, and *taro* patches were scattered in the uplands. Five *heiau* were located in the vicinity. Today only Keaiwa Heiau remains in 'Aiea Heights within the State Park reservation. A visit to this *heiau* is instructive. The visitor will find that ancient customs are still observed as many *ti* leaf-wrapped gifts are still offered to the gods. The other four *heiau* have been erased by sugarcane cultivation followed with housing developments.

'Aiea was the site of an epochal battle in December 1784 between the forces of Kalanikupule, ruler of O'ahu, and those of his uncle, Kaeokulani, ruler of Kaua'i. Kalanikupule's forces were victorious only to be defeated the following year by the forces of Kamehameha I in the battle of the Nu'uanu Pali. Kaeokulani was killed and a major threat to the conquering plans of Kamehameha was thereby removed.

The battle in 'Aiea was of historical significance for other reasons, too. It was the first in which *haole* gunners participated and during which some were killed. Marc Amara (Marc the armorer), a renegade ship's blacksmith, served as a gunner for Kaeokulani and at least eight Caucasian seamen from the ships *Jackal* and *Prince Lee Boo* served with Kalanikupule's forces. To place this battle in historical perspective, it happened during President George Washington's (1732-1799) second term of office.

It is difficult today to imagine that most of the lands occupied by Hickam Air Force Base, Honolulu International Airport, Pearl Harbor Naval Station, and the communities Halawa Heights, 'Aiea, and Pearl City were blanketed with cultivated fields of sugarcane as recently as 1947. Yet, there are those alive today who worked for, or remember, the now-gone Honolulu Plantation Company.

Investment prospects on O'ahu greatly improved following the annexation of the Republic of Hawaii by the United States in 1898. The threat of tariffs being levied by the United States on Hawaiian sugar imports was removed forever by the annexation. Capitalists were quick to see the advantages in this development, and Suessmann and Wurmser, owners of the mainland S. & W. food store chain, in 1898 incorporated the Honolulu Plantation Company to exploit the situation. The company leased 8,000 acres in and around Pearl Harbor and erected a modern sugarmill in 'Aiea only seven miles from downtown Honolulu. The plantation was served by thirty-one miles of a 36-inch narrow gauge railroad system that hauled harvested cane to the 'Aiea mill. The sprawling plantation occupied lands from the location of today's Honolulu International Airport to as far west as today's Pearl City.

This plantation was unique in Hawai'i because, beginning in 1906, it refined its harvests, and those of the Waimanalo Sugar Company, to produce sugar for local consumption. The rest of the plantations shipped their raw sugar product to mainland refineries. The 'Aiea refinery supplied sugar for bottlers and pineapple packers as well as for local domestic sales.

The heyday for the plantation was 1930 when 31,720 tons of sugar were produced and refined at the 'Aiea mill. Over 500 company-owned cottages for 4,000 workers and dependents were distributed in camps throughout the plantation. The plantation maintained a fully-staffed hospital for its residents and struggled to keep a separate and independent identity despite being a mere seven miles from metropolitan Honolulu. Amenities on site included a church, a temple, a Japanese language school, baseball fields, and a plantation library. Despite all, the manager complained bitterly about labor recruiters visiting the camps during the periodic labor shortages in Honolulu.

The plantation surrendered lands in bits and pieces to the federal government in the years after 1900. Finally, in 1935, the plantation gave up the last of the Pu'uloa lands to the government, which intended to build Hickam Field at the location. A plantation village was erased by the airport construction and thousands of acres of sugarcane were surrendered along with a part of the plantation railroad. Additional government land acquisition during World War II reduced the remaining plantation lands to the point that sugarcane cultivation was no longer profitable.

Alvah A. Scott managed the plantation from 1928 to 1939 when he left to become chief executive of the Hawaiian Telephone Company.

Scott was a humane and much-respected manager who saw the plantation through its most profitable years. His career is a is a good example of the way prominent young *kama'aina* were promoted and advanced in the early twentieth century. In 1920 he succeeded his father, pioneer Hilo businessman John A. Scott (1848-1925), as manager of the Hilo Sugar Company. He then became an executive with plantation owner C. Brewer & Company. An elementary school located in 'Aiea Heights is named in Alvah A. Scott's memory.

In 1947 then-owner C. Brewer & Co. shut down the plantation and dismantled and sold the mill machinery to a Philippine operator. The railroad equipment was sold to neighboring Ewa Plantation. The Honolulu Plantation Company became a memory.

Vestiges of 'Aiea's sugarcane heritage remain despite the overwhelming urban developments. In 1972 a modern multi-story headquarters for the Hawaiian Sugar Planters' Association (now named Hawaii Agriculture Research Center), was built next to the C & H sugar refinery. A stop at this location, on 'Aiea Heights Drive inland from H-1 Freeway, rewards the inquisitive. A primitive stone sugarmill is displayed prominently in front of this building. Two large cylindrical stone grinders were found in the ruins of the old sugarmill at Kualoa Ranch and moved to 'Aiea for this display. This kind of mill was powered by animals and fell out of use before 1850. It is fitting and proper that the home of modern sugarcane farming technology and this ancient mill share this site on the lands of what was once Hawai'i's most advanced sugar producing plantation. It's all history now.

The refinery, updated through the years, survived until 1995 when it shut down. The building was a long-time landmark standing at the original 'Aiea sugarmill location. Until 1998, when it was demolished, the C & H logo served as a landmark that could easily be seen from Highway H-1.

The Oahu Sugar Company ground its last crop in 1995. The sugarmill's chimney remains intact and, perched as it is on a hillock, dominates the former plantation community of Waipahu. Waipahu's story amplifies that which will be seen exhibited in the museum and on the grounds of Hawaii's Plantation Village.

WAIPAHU

O'ahu's Highway H-1 passes through the fringes of the town of Waipahu on its way from Honolulu to the west coast of the island. When you look toward Pearl Harbor while passing through Waipahu you see the chimney of the sugarmill of the Oahu Sugar Company in the foreground. The town owes its existence to this mill and when it closed down in 1995, an vital era passed for its people.

Before Capt. James Cook first visited Hawai'i in 1778 there was no community named Waipahu. The location was in the *ahupua'a* of Waikele within the *moku* of 'Ewa. Waikele was the home of numerous Native Hawaiians spread out from the mountains to the shore at the West Loch of Pearl Harbor. Two *heiau,* now destroyed, were located near the present location of the sugarmill. A free-flowing spring gushed nearby. Waipahu owes its name to this spring; *wai* means "water" and *pahu* means "rushing forth." Native legends abound concerning this spring.

Benjamin F. Dillingham took the first steps that resulted in the community of Waipahu when, in the late 1880s, he leased thousands of acres of James Campbell's land in Ewa and Waialua Districts. By 1890 he had built his O.R.& L. railroad from Honolulu to Kahuku. He encouraged the formation of Ewa Plantation Company, Waialua Agricultural Company, and Kahuku Plantation Company, partially on the lands he had leased from Campbell, to create a supply of sugar to be hauled by his railroad. He wasn't done with his promotions, and in 1897 encouraged the formation of Oahu Sugar Company on the Waikele lands he had leased from Campbell.

Oahu Sugar Company subleased lands from Dillingham and leased additional lands from the John Papa I'i Estate, Bernice Pauahi Bishop Estate, and Robinson Estate to become a 12,000 acre plantation, one of the largest on O'ahu. The vast operation was served by fifty-five miles of 36-inch narrow-gauge railroad until replaced by trucks in 1951. Sugar was transported fourteen miles to the Honolulu docks by the O.R.& L. until the railroad shut down in 1947.

In the plantation's heyday, the 1930s, over 5,000 workers and dependents lived in over 1,000 company-owned houses distributed among several dispersed camps. The mill community, Waipahu, was the site of a company hospital serviced by two physicians and several nurses, two of whom made regular visits to the outlying camps. A movie theater and store were operated by the company in Waipahu.

The workers came in waves. First the Portuguese, then Japanese, and finally, Koreans, Puerto Ricans, and Filipinos. Most of them stayed in Hawai'i and helped form the ethnic mix of modern-day Hawai'i. By 1946 the workers of all races banded together under a common cause and, led by the International Longshoremen's and Warehousemen's Union (ILWU), struck for and won lasting concessions from their sugar company employers. It was the first such interracial cooperative effort in Hawai'i.

Oahu Sugar Company was the last of Dillingham's plantation promotions on O'ahu because it was the most difficult to supply with irrigation. Much of the cultivated uplands were 500 to 1,000 feet above the water table. When heavy-duty steam pumps became available, a way was found to lift well water some 300 to 600 feet in the quantities required. Some of the pumps were located in sumps 250 to 300 feet below the surface. Sugar is a very thirsty crop. Each pound of sugar produced requires one ton of water to sustain growth of the parent sugarcane to maturity.

By 1913 the limits of pumped well water were reached and further growth was impossible. The Waiahole Water Company, a subsidiary of Oahu Sugar Company, was formed to construct a system to collect water on the windward slopes of the distant Ko'olau mountain range, and transport it via a tunnel through the mountains to the fields in Waikele. By 1916 this system was delivering between 100 and 150 million gallons of water daily to the thirsty plantation fields.

In 1917 the company surrendered its Ford Island lease to the government. The War Department established Luke Field on the western side of the island, and the Navy Department established a seaplane airdrome on the eastern side. Luke Field was abandoned when the Army completed Hickam Field in 1939 and the Navy took complete control of the island.

In 1970 Oahu Sugar Company added lands of the Ewa Plantation Company when that plantation closed. For twenty-five years these land additions enabled Oahu Sugar Company to maintain a viable 10,000 acres or so of sugarcane while at the same time surrendering thousands of acres to urban growth. The population of the land in and around Waipahu now numbers about 30,000 people, and Waipahu has become a bedroom community for Honolulu workers.

In 1988 JMB Realty Corporation purchased Oahu Sugar Company from Amfac, Inc. In August 1993 Amfac/JMB-Hawaii announced that it was shutting down Oahu Sugar Company after the 1995 harvest because of unprofitable operation in recent years, and because renewal of certain leases was uncertain. Some 370 sugar workers were affected by the closing.

Reminders of Hawai'i's sugar heritage survive in Waipahu. In 1973 the State and County purchased over forty acres of land across from the mill and next to Waipahu Street to be used for the Waipahu Cultural Garden Park. After several years of hard work by volunteers, this park has matured as the location of Hawaii's Plantation Village. This facility is must-visit for those interested in Hawai'i's plantation past. An excellent museum contains exhibits and murals describing the growth of the sugar industry and the people who worked in it. Nearby are reconstructions of plantation houses, buildings, and a temple, all properly furnished, that illustrate plantation living from early 1800s to post-World War II. Several of the docents are elderly retired plantation workers who are generous with answers to your questions. This fine museum does much to perpetuate the sugar industry's heritage in Hawai'i and has outlived the operation of the sugar mill in Waipahu.

One interesting exhibit is the plantation steam locomotive and attached cane-haul railroad car positioned on a length of narrow-gauge railroad track. This authentic exhibit was salvaged from the

Restored and furnished 1935-era plantation house among those displayed in Waipahu at Hawaii's Plantation Village. Replicas of housing and buildings from several eras are on display at the village. *(W. H. Dorrance)*

artifacts of the Oahu Sugar Company and is one of very few pieces of plantation railroad equipment surviving from the pre-1952 era.

Replica of an authentic grass hut of the kind inhabited by an early 1800s sugarcane worker that is exhibited at Hawaii's Plantation Village in Waipahu. This is surely one of a very few such grass huts displayed in Hawaii. *(W. H. Dorrance)*

THE O.R. & L. AND THE HAWAIIAN RAILWAY SOCIETY

Volunteers of the nonprofit Hawaiian Railway Society have been working hard for over 20 years to restore and preserve artifacts of O'ahu's post-1878 history. The Kingdom of Hawai'i was ruled by its seventh monarch, King David Kalakaua, from 1874 to 1891. King Kalakaua ushered telephones and electric power into his kingdom. In 1878 he signed the Railway Act into law, providing for eminent domain to create railroad rights-of-way. King Kalakaua accelerated the march of progress with the stroke of his pen.

Local businessman Benjamin F. Dillingham saw the opportunities created by this act. In 1885 he obtained an option to lease much of the vast acreage owned by businessman James Campbell on the west and northeast sides of O'ahu. In his eyes this uncultivated land was ripe for development.

Dillingham formed a corporation and tried to sell stock to raise money to purchase a 50-year lease to the land. He planned to sublease the land to sugar planters to create a need for the railroad he planned to build. On his first trip to London, Dillingham failed to arrange an underwriting, so he revised his thinking. Instead, he would sell bonds to raise money to build a railroad. This, in turn, would make his land lease option more valuable. With this successful approach, he began to construct the Oahu Railway & Land Company railroad in 1886.

Dillingham built the railroad from Honolulu to the northeast shore of O'ahu at Kahuku from 1886 to 1899. The 36-inch gauge railroad turned into a gold-plated cash cow as the number of plantations in the area grew. Sublease payments by Ewa Plantation to Dillingham covered his payments to Campbell.

Railroad tycoon Benjamin Franklin Dillingham (1844-1918) *(Hawai'i State Archives)*

Prosperous before Dillingham's death in 1918, the O.R.& L. railroad lived on to enjoy its best years in the 20th century. During World War II it hauled passengers, freight, and war materiel around the clock. However, by 1947, the railroad's time had passed. The highways were improved and the railroad could no longer compete with motor trucks. The last train to the North Shore ran in 1947, shutting down most of the O.R.& L. railroad forever.

After the railroad ceased operations, the Navy continued to use the rails from Pearl Harbor to Lualualei near Nanakuli to haul ammunition. Eventually, however, the roadbed deteriorated and the bridges came in need of major repairs. Therefore, in 1968, the Navy abandoned its use of this last stretch of rails.

Train made up of former O.R.& L. rolling stock located in the Hawaiian Railway Society yard in 'Ewa. *(W. H. Dorrance)*

About this time, the late John Knaus, then a retired employee of the Navy facility at Lualualei, organized an enthusiastic group of railroad buffs who were determined to preserve vestiges of the old railroad. In 1970 they formed the Hawaiian Railway Society to preserve Hawaiian railway equipment, to rehabilitate what remained of O'ahu's railroad, and to establish a railway museum. The Society soon became the 100th affiliated chapter of the nonprofit National Railway Historical Society.

In 1978 the Society leased a site in 'Ewa from Campbell Estate for use as a railroad yard where repairs and renovations could take place. The Society's volunteers were soon hard at work laying track in the yard and gathering railroad equipment from sundry locations in the Islands. Situated next to the Barbers Point Naval Air Station fence at the end of Renton Road, the yard contains repair sheds, an office and gift shop, parking tracks and exhibits. The former O.R.& L. tracks are located between the yard and the Barbers Point reservation fence.

For years Bishop Museum exhibited a locomotive and coaches which were donated to the museum after the railroad shut down. The museum loaned these items to the Society which is restoring the equipment. The Society obtained two locomotives, both in need of restoration, from Ewa Plantation and the Oahu Sugar Company. The Army and the Navy have contributed rolling stock. The Society's volunteers are faced with years of restoration work.

The State of Hawaii owns the right-of-way from Aloha Stadium through Waipahu and on up the coast to Lualualei. This 40-foot wide easement is reserved for electric, gas, sewer and water lines. Railroad tracks remain on the portion of the corridor from Fort Weaver Road to Lualualei and are listed in the National Register of Historic Places. Society volunteers have restored the five miles of tracks from the yard in 'Ewa to the golf course at Ko Olina to usable condition, and on these tracks the Society conducts train rides every Sunday and on special occasions.

A former Navy diesel-electric locomotive pulls the excursion trains. Converted flat cars equipped with side rails, benches and some top covers carry passengers. An excursion train includes as many as six cars. The pleasant one-hour round-trip yields views of former cane fields, Barbers Point Naval Air Station, old Fort

Barrette, Campbell Industrial Park Harbor, and part of the golf course at Ko Olina. An excursion train can accommodate up to 175 passengers.

The Society has ambitious plans to extend the operating railroad southeast to Waipahu Cultural Garden Park and north to Nanakuli. This will require putting down track from Fort Weaver Road to Waipahu, and the renovation of track from the golf course at Ko

Former Ewa Plantation Company locomotive displayed in the rail yard of the Hawaiian Railway Society in Ewa. *(W. H. Dorrance)*

Olina to Nanakuli. The Society also plans to build a replica of the O.R.& L. railway station, which was once located at the terminus in Iwilei (replaced in 1925 by the existing building on N. King Street) in the Ewa Yard to provide a ticket office, snack bar and restrooms. In addition, the Society is also planning a railroad museum and a complex of repair shops.

None of the steam locomotives in the Society's possession are in running condition. All need new boilers and other expensive repairs. The restoration of two O.R.& L. passenger coaches and several steam locomotives is currently underway. The restoration of Walter Dillingham's elegant parlor car has been completed. While gifts, donations, dues and the proceeds from excursion train rides cover Society operating expenses with modest reserves, additional revenues will be required if the Society is to realize all of its plans.

When asked why much of the Society's former O.R.& L. equipment was in such run-down condition, a longtime Society member and volunteer pointed out, "You have to realize that some of this equipment is almost one-hundred years old. It has been forty-five years since the railroad shut down. The equipment has been exposed to the elements since then. O.R.& L. had a roundhouse to house the locomotives, and the equipment received regular maintenance that ended when the O.R.& L. shut down."

The Society's monthly newsletter is now in its third decade, and the enthusiasm of its members and volunteers remains strong. Society members look forward to the day when their completed restoration project will enable everyone to ride in a steam-locomotive train that played a vital role in O'ahu's economic and historical development.

❖   ❖   ❖

Look over the air station's chain link fence toward the ocean before leaving the railroad society's premises. What you see are the southeastern grounds of the large Barbers Point Naval Air Station reservation. The land between the road on the other side of the fence and the golf course is covered with a *kiawe* tree and shrub jungle interspersed with decaying macadam hard stands, taxi ways, and runways. Access is currently limited to military personnel and those with gate passes, but that will soon change. The government announced in 1994 that the naval units based in the reservation would be moved elsewhere and the large reservation turned over to the State of Hawai'i. If so, you will be able to use the golf course and explore the artifacts left over from the long-gone Marine Corps Air Station-Ewa that once occupied the land on the other side of the fence. The story of this station is a piece of O'ahu's history.

MCAS-Ewa

Barbers Point is a peninsula which juts out to the southwest from the island of O'ahu. The naval station located on this peninsula is enclosed within a security fence, covers a vast area, and is more than an air field. The outer reaches of the former plantation town of Ewa abut the security fence on the inland side of the base.

A golf course is laid out on the reservation and far from the naval station's runways in an area lying in the direction of Honolulu. There is a macadam road which winds through the middle of the course. During a drive along this road you will sense that the road is turning into either an old taxiway or an old runway.

Soon you encounter an even more interesting sight. Just off the road in the *kiawe* jungle is a large concrete-quarterspherical shelter.

Kiawe trees cover the backside. A decaying macadam path similar to the road leads to it. It is deserted and obviously neglected.

Looking around you can find several more such structures scattered about in the *kiawe* forest. Few have been in use for years judging from the signs of neglect. If you explore further, you will locate over fifty of these curious structures. All have crumbling macadam paths leading to them.

On the outskirts of this forest, in the 'Ewa plantation direction, you come across what could only be a crumbling old runway. The paths from the concrete shelters led to this runway. You have stumbled across the remnants of an abandoned military airfield. What was it and why was it abandoned? These are the remains of the Marine Corps Air Station-Ewa (MCAS-Ewa). This station played a key role in World War II and was deactivated in 1949.

One of fifty-some quartersphere airplane shelters distributed through the *kiawe* forest within the Barbers Point NAS and near the former location of abandoned NAS-Ewa. *(W. H. Dorrance)*

In the early 1930s the U.S. Navy pioneered a strategy involving the use of large, lighter-than-air, rigid airships. These dirigibles were so large they actually carried their own fighter planes in an on-board hangar. There were two of them, the *Akron* and the *Macon*. They required mooring masts to tether them when they were grounded.

The Navy's strategy called for the *Akron* to support the Atlantic Fleet, and the *Macon* to operate in the Pacific. A base in Hawai'i was needed for the *Macon* so the Navy purchased some 4,000 acres in 'Ewa from the Campbell Estate to provide for it. The area selected was just west of Ewa Town.

Soon a small runway and a mooring mast were constructed by the Navy on the 'Ewa site. All was ready to receive the mighty *Macon*.

However, use of NAS-Ewa as a dirigible base was not to be. Both the *Akron* and the *Macon* were destroyed in fierce storms during the 1930s. Along with them went the concept of using large dirigibles, and in 1939 the Navy turned the small 'Ewa field over to the Marine Corps.

The Marines enlarged the field a little and stationed two squadrons of scout bombers there. It was lazy duty at a remote tropical station during the time just before World War II. The little station was some twenty miles from Honolulu, about an hour's ride on the train going in from 'Ewa and forty-five minutes in a car.

In early 1941 the U.S. was not at war. However, times were tense as the Germans had already defeated France in Europe and

Mooring mast erected in the 1930s at the NAS-Ewa air field to tether the dirigible *Macon*. The *Macon* perished in a 1935 Pacific storm but the mooring mast lived on as a control tower until demolished after World War II. (*National Archives*)

the Japanese were making war in China. It seemed only sensible that the U.S. forces in Hawai'i take extra security precautions. According to official military policy at the time, the number-one perceived threat was ground-based sabotage. Therefore, at MCAS-Ewa, precautions included gathering the aircraft in tight groups when they were idle on the ground so that fewer sentries were required to guard them. Thus on the weekends they were carefully aligned wing-tip to wing-tip and nose to tail in one easily-guarded grouping.

The Japanese attack of December 7, 1941 was probably one of the most successful military operations in history. It was a well-organized attack involving torpedo bombers, dive bombers, horizontal bombers and fighters. The fighters supplied "air suppression" or destruction of defensive fighters. Air bases at Wheeler, Kane'ohe, 'Ewa, Hickam, Bellows, and Ford Island were all strafed by Japanese fighters, some immediately before the Pearl Harbor attack. It being Sunday, most of the planes were grounded and were destroyed by strafers who made their passes at no more than fifteen to thirty feet altitude.

At 'Ewa it was "duck soup" for the Japanese as the planes were conveniently assembled in a tight grouping. Two passes were all it took to destroy thirty-three of forty-nine airplanes on the ground. This occurred some minutes before the Pearl Harbor attack began.

After the attack, the U.S. forces in Hawai'i regrouped. MCAS-Ewa was assigned the role of defending Pearl Harbor in the event of another attack. Such was the desperation of our position that the Marine fighter pilots at MCAS-Ewa were assigned obsolete Brewster Buffalo fighters. These miserably underpowered fighter planes were the best available at the time.

The Brewsters were dispersed among the *kiawe* trees and some were protected by makeshift sandbag revetments. It was a temporary measure until more permanent shelters could be made. Of course in those desperate days of early 1942, all U.S. services were clamoring for more and better fighter planes. MCAS-Ewa waited its turn. In

Brewster Buffalo fighter plane concealed among *kiawe* trees at MCAS-Ewa in 1942. These underpowered planes were replaced with more modern aircraft late in 1942. *(National Archives)*

the meantime, construction of more permanent concrete shelters was begun. These are the shelters found at the side of the road through the Barbers Point golf course.

Finally MCAS-Ewa got decent fighter planes, Grumman F4F Wildcats. These little fighters fit nicely into the new shelters. If they had been in such shelters on December 7, 1941 they would undoubtedly all have survived the attack.

MCAS-Ewa grew in size and became a key transfer station for Marine air groups coming and going in the Pacific. Eventually the Grumman F4Fs were replaced with the higher-powered Grumman F6F Hellcats that still fit in the revetments. Then, at the war's end, the F6F's were augmented with the new gull-winged Chance Vought F4U Corsairs. The shelters were getting a little tight as the size of fighter planes grew.

Adjacent Barber's Point NAS was started during WW II and had grown in size until its environs overlapped those of MCAS-Ewa. By 1952 the Navy had given up its Kane'ohe base to the Marines from MCAS-Ewa, and MCAS-Ewa was closed down and left to the *kiawe* jungle. The jungle is reclaiming what was wrenched from it some sixty years ago.

Some of the land of MCAS-Ewa serves on. The Barber's Point golf course uses a good deal of what was runway. Six or so of the quarter-sphere shelters adjacent to the course are used for stables since the vast air station reservation has much room for riding trails within the security fence.

It is unlikely that the young horseback riders can relate to the history of the surroundings. The story of MCAS-Ewa will no doubt be forgotten history when the last veteran dies and what's left of the station is bulldozed away.

A visit to old Fort Barrette is next on your tour of 'Ewa. This leg of the tour is optional because currently the fort's reservation is secure behind a locked gate, and arrangements must be made with the City and County of Honolulu's Parks and Recreation Department to gain access. The City and County's Ewa Complex Manager will accommodate you. However, you can see something of the site by driving by it on the access road to the main gate of Barbers Point Naval Air Station, Fort Barrette Road.

Fort Barrette was one of the shortest-lived Coast Artillery forts on O'ahu.

FORT BARRETTE

The story begins with the conclusion of the Washington Naval Conference of 1921-1922. France, Italy, Japan, Great Britain, and the United States agreed to suspend capital ship construction for ten years and to reduce capital ship numbers to mutually agreed upon limits. The United States had to cease production of, or scrap, fifteen battleships and battle cruisers. As a result, the U.S. Navy had a surplus of 16-inch guns on its hands. Some of these guns were turned over to the Army for coast defense, and O'ahu got a pair of them.

The knoll located adjacent to Fort Barrette Road is the site of long-deactivated Fort Barrette. Originally called Kapolei Military Reservation, construction began in July 1931 to prepare sites for mounting two of the great 16-inch guns made surplus by the 1922 treaty. These enormous guns could hurl a 2,240-lb. projectile to a maximum range of some twenty-five miles. Almost all of O'ahu fell within that range from the carefully-chosen site at Kapolei. The two guns were installed so they had a 360-degree traverse. Within a circle of twenty-five miles radius no enemy could be safe from the guns at the Kapolei site.

Moving these heavy guns from the docks at Pearl Harbor to the reservation was a challenge. The great barrels of the guns with their cradles weighed hundreds of tons. The engineers were faced with

Transporting a Navy 16-inch gun to Fort Barrette via the O.R.& L. It was a major project to transport these heavy guns from the Pearl Harbor docks to Fort Barrette. *(J. Conde Collection)*

moving heavy and unwieldy objects, and Kapolei was a remote site in those days. In the 1930s no convenient heavy-duty freeway ran near the site, as Highway H-1 does now. The now long-gone O.R.& L. railroad came to the rescue. Tracks of the main line ran near the site as they wound their way north from Waipahu. It was a simple matter to put a spur line down to service the Army's Kapolei site.

Special railroad cars were required to spread the load of the heavy guns while being transported on the O.R.& L.'s narrow gauge tracks. Six-and twelve-wheel trucks were used to distribute the load. A crane-bearing wrecking car accompanied each move. Despite the precautions, the load of one of the guns shifted en route to Kapolei, necessitating use of the wrecker to reset the load properly on the rails. It was a nerve-wracking operation to move the guns and the parts of their carriages to Kapolei.

On August 11, 1934 the two guns were emplaced, and the site was turned over to the Army's Coast Artillery.

With activation of the battery, its name was changed to Fort Barrette. Brig. Gen. John D. Barrette (1862-1934) had commanded the Hawaii Coast Artillery District from 1921 to 1924. In keeping with Coast Artillery traditions, the two guns within the fort were designated a battery. The name of Brig. Gen. Henry J. Hatch (unk.-1931) was given to the battery henceforth to be known as "Battery Hatch." General Hatch as a young officer had commanded a unit at Fort Kamehameha in 1913.

Fort Barrette was strafed by the Japanese on December 7, 1941. That must have suggested to military intelligence that a Japanese landing on O'ahu was imminent. Even today the Fort Barrette location

One of two Navy 16-inch guns emplaced at Fort Barrette. The sugarcane field forward of the gun is now occupied by the community of Kapolei. Both guns were casemated in 1942-1945. (U. S. Army Museum of Hawai'i)

is clearly visible to airline passengers who know where to look on the approach to Honolulu International Airport. The attacking Japanese aircraft could not have missed sighting the fort with its two exposed guns.

In 1942, after the attack, the Army begun to casemate (i.e. provide overhead protection) the two guns with their magazines and auxiliaries. This construction surrounded the guns with 8-to 12-foot thick protective concrete cover. Casemating of the guns meant giving up their unrestricted 360-degree field of fire. However, the guns still covered the approaches to Pearl Harbor, and safety of the exposed guns was deemed to be more important than all-around fire.

In addition to casemating the guns, the plotting, electrical power generators, and switchboard rooms were covered with concrete and earth. The garrison was supported by an on-site post exchange.

A dedicated narrow-gauge railroad system transported heavy supplies, projectiles, and powder throughout the fort. The railway lines ran between the two guns and around the periphery of the fort. The gauge matched the 36-inch gauge of the O.R.& L. railroad and the Army had its own inventory of railway cars and switch engines.

The interior corridors of the two underground casemates are each branched by five protected chambers. Two are projectile rooms, two are powder rooms, and one is a general storeroom. All were connected to the guns by the fort's railway system. Four concrete powder and shell magazine buildings were distributed around the grounds of the fort and served by the fort's railway system. The fort is contained within a fenced 38-acre plot of land which occupies the knoll.

No remnants of the elaborate fort railway system survive today. Also, of course, the guns and their mounts have been removed.

Empty casemate of one of the two 16-inch guns emplaced at Fort Barrette. Casemating was done in 1942-45. A radar was installed to point the guns when visibility obscured optical sighting or when night fell. *(W. H. Dorrance)*

However, it would take a major demolition effort to remove the tons of concrete that make up the present remains of Fort Barrette.

The outer reaches of the fort were guarded by strategically-located concrete pillboxes placed on the sides of the knoll overlooking the surrounding Ewa plains. Riflemen and machine gunners manned these dank and musty pillboxes during times of threat. In those days the fort was surrounded by sugarcane fields whose Japanese workers were regarded as potential enemy sympathizers.

As with most U.S. Army Coast Artillery forts, Fort Barrette was deactivated with the end of World War II. Modern missiles and nuclear weapons made long-range coast defense guns an anachronism, and a military era has passed. In 1972 City and County of Honolulu took over ownership of the thirty-eight acres of Fort Barrette and is currently in the slow process of converting the land into a city park.

The visit to Fort Barrette completes your tour of 'Ewa *moku*. It's time to move north along the west coast to the historic former sugar plantation community of Wai'anae.

Chapter Twelve

'Ewa to Wai'anae

THE WEST SIDE of O'ahu receives little rainfall. Sugar plantations were slow to appear because of this desert-like environment. Establishment of sugarcane plantations awaited the 1890s installation of powerful steam pumps that were able to lift vast quantities of water from the underground aquifer. Today the plantations are gone and lands bordering the shore of West O'ahu are occupied by small farms and settlements, many of which are populated with Native Hawaiian families. The beaches are coveted by surfers and family picnickers. Here is the story of the former plantation community of Wai'anae.

WAI'ANAE

Wai'anae is the large *moku* that extends from Nanakuli on the west coast of O'ahu north to Ka'ena Point. Today, residents are most likely to associate the name with the largest town in the district that is located almost at midpoint of the district's coast line. The boundaries of the ancient *moku* included eight *ahupua'a* of which one was also called Wai'anae.

The leeward side of every Hawaiian island is dry and parched because the prevailing trade winds drop their moisture when encountering the mountainous slopes that line the eastern coasts of each island. It seldom rains in Wai'anae. Nevertheless, archeological evidence suggests that Wai'anae supported a large population of natives before the arrival of Europeans. In years past, Bishop Museum archeologists located nineteen *heiau* in Wai'anae *moku*. Of these, only three survive to be identified on modern maps. Such has been the march of progress in Wai'anae.

The ancient culture in Wai'anae followed the traditional Hawaiian pattern of fishing villages at the shore with terraced *taro* patches in the mountainous foothills. Those growing *taro* in the uplands exchanged their harvests for the fish caught by those living near the shore. However, Wai'anae differed from the Windward O'ahu *moku* in that the lands in between the shore and foothills were parched and neglected and too dry for agricultural pursuits.

The settlement of Wai'anae is reputed to be the location of the first coconut planting in Hawai'i. According to legend, the great Hawaiian navigator Pokai planted the first trees there following a voyage into the southwestern Pacific centuries before the first contact with Europeans. It is comforting to observe that remnants of such a grove survive and that the English explorer Capt. George Vancouver reported seeing a grove in that location in his journals. Vancouver spent the winters of 1792, 1793, and 1794 exploring the islands.

For centuries the settlement of Wai'anae, with its sheltered bay, served as a point of departure for canoes bound for Kaua'i. In 1796, after Kamehameha I had completed his capture of O'ahu and the southern islands, he paused at Wai'anae with his warrior fleet preparatory to moving on to capture dominion over Kaua'i and Ni'ihau. He carried his war god Kuka'ilimoku ashore for a religious ceremony at a nearby *heiau*, then prepared for a midnight departure for Kaua'i. It was not to be. A storm came up after the canoes departed and several were swamped in mid-channel. Kamehameha returned to the shelter of Pokai Bay and delayed plans to invade Kaua'i for years thereafter. He never did reach Kaua'i.

Following the Great Mahele of 1848-1850, the kingdom retained most of the lands of Wai'anae *moku*. The dwindling number of Native Hawaiians continued to fish at the shore and farm in the uplands. In 1850 the American Mission in Hawai'i (Congregational Church) ordained Stephen Waimalu and installed him as independent pastor of the church at Wai'anae. It was only the third such ordination of a Native Hawaiian.

By 1860 Frank Paul Manini (1823-unk.) was ranching in most of the leased lands of the district. His cattle, wild pigs, and goats roamed the flat lands. Manini was one of twenty-three known children of pioneer settler Francisco de Paula Marin, loyal follower of Kings Kamehameha I, II, and III.

Sometime before 1878 James Isaac Dowsett purchased title to vast lands in the district. In 1878 three enterprising sugar planters,

Judge Herman A. Widemann, George Norton Wilcox (1839-1933), and Albert Spencer Wilcox (1844-1919), leased the lands and planted sugarcane. They incorporated the enterprise as Waianae Company in 1880 and a new era began.

All three planters were pioneers from Kaua'i. George and Albert Wilcox were sons of missionary Abner Wilcox (1808-1869) who had arrived in Hawai'i in 1837 with the eighth company of American missionaries. Widemann was perhaps the most interesting of the three. He was a German national who arrived in Hawai'i before 1849 as a teenage sailor on a whaling vessel. After a fling in California during the 1849 gold rush he returned to Kaua'i to settle down, successively, as bookkeeper at Lihue plantation, independent planter (who accumulated the lands of Kaua'i's Grove Farm plantation), sheriff of the island, and District Judge. Widemann was a staunch monarchist and defended Queen Lili'uokalani during her misdirected trial for treason. Widemann sold Grove Farm Plantation to George N. Wilcox in 1870.

Waianae Landing in Pokai Bay circa 1900. Until the O.R.& L. railroad was completed to Wai'anae, all shipments to and from the Wai'anae plantation were lightered between the landing and coasters anchored offshore. *(Bishop Museum)*

The Wai'anae plantation occupied some 2,000 acres in Lualualei, Wai'anae, and Makaha Valleys. While it was never a large plantation by modern standards, it was one of the first and last to be served by a plantation railroad. Some fifteen miles of 30-inch narrow-gauge railroad delivered harvested cane to the mill. All the sugar was shipped by inter-island vessels to Honolulu departing from Waianae Landing until the O.R.& L. railroad was extended to Wai'anae and beyond in 1889.

The coaster S.S. *W.G. Hall,* 386 tons displacenent, serving the Inter-Island Steamship Co. on the Honolulu-Lahaina—Kona and Honolulu-Kaua'i runs circa 1900. She dropped anchor off Waianae Landing when on the Honolulu-Kaua'i-run. *(Hawaii State Archives)*

Waianae plantation was noted for the humane treatment of employees. During the 1930s much of the plantation's earnings went into improving company-owned housing and facilities for workers and dependents. Following the importation of Japanese workers the makeup changed from Native Hawaiians to a significant fraction of Japanese. In 1905 a Japanese language school was established in Wai'anae as a reflection of the population mix.

The J. M. Dowsett Estate sold the plantation to American Factors (now Amfac/JMB-Hawai'i) in 1931. After the O.R.& L. shut down in 1947, the plantation ceased operations and an era for Wai'anae came to an end.

Today the Wai'anae District is the location of Hawaiian homelands and homesteads. The region is still hot and dusty, but the beaches are inviting, fishing and surfing are popular, and progress is being made in enlarging the capacity of the water supply and sewerage, and improving the roads.

The lands north of Wai'anae to Ka'ena Point are sparsely settled but the fishing offshore is rewarding. Makua Valley, on the *mauka* or inland side of the road, has been used as a military training area since World War II. Before that it was occupied by a cattle ranch. Today it is difficult as well as forbidden to drive north beyond Yokohama Beach to Ka'ena Point.

KA'ENA POINT

Legend has it that the demi-god Maui was determined to unite Kaua'i and O'ahu into one land mass. He stationed himself at Ka'ena Point and cast his wonderful hook towards Kaua'i to grapple the island's foundation. With one magnificent tug, his grapple pulled in the sea-boulder now shown on today's maps as Pohaku o Kaua'i. The island of Kaua'i remained where it had been and Maui moved on to other pursuits.

Ka'ena is the name of the westernmost *ahupua'a* in the *moku* of Waialua and is the westernmost location on O'ahu. From its heights you can see Kaua'i. The Point plays a legendary role in Native Hawaiian traditions. It was believed in ancient times that the souls of the dying departed O'ahu from there. Ka'ena Point remains an appropriate location for this spiritual departure to this day. Few strangers can violate the security of the locality that is now sealed off by landslides on the Wai'anae Coast side, and a substantial gate on the Waialua side.

When Benjamin F. Dillingham, in 1890, extended his O.R.& L. railroad from Honolulu to Kahuku, his construction crew was faced with a challenge at Ka'ena Point. There was little more than a rutted and rocky trail around the Point to be traversed by the railroad. The right-of-way had to be cut through volcanic rock and a sharp 150-degree turn was necessary. The excavators did the job but the railroad was faced with a bottleneck at the Point. All trains slowed down and crept around it while passengers craned their necks for a glimpse of Kaua'i. It was a dramatic passage. The ocean washed the rocks lining the shore just below the tracks.

The trail that now passes around the Point was left by the uprooted tracks of the long-departed O.R.& L. The tsunami of April 1, 1946 wiped out a length of track in Mokule'ia, motor trucks had replaced much of the railroad hauling, and prospects for the railroad were grim. The damage done by the tsunami was the last straw and in 1947 the railroad shut down.

In the early 1920s the Army acquired most of the land overlooking the point for a military reservation. Two long-range guns had been emplaced at Fort Weaver, and a fire control station was needed at Ka'ena Point in order to direct cannon fire and report fall of shot near the point. In 1923 a fire control station, known as "Station

S," was constructed in the heights above the point and connected by telephone with the gun emplacements back at the fort at the entrance to Pearl Harbor. The station is a small, rectangular, covered concrete structure entered through a manhole in the roof. Another such station was built just below Station S after the two 16-inch long-range guns

One of two 16-inch rifles emplaced at Fort Weaver in 1922 and removed by 1950. These great guns could hurl a 2,340 lb. projectile to a range of 28 miles and covered the approaches to every beach on O'ahu. Observers at Ka'ena Point Station S determined target coordinates in that vicinity. *(U.S. Army Museum of Hawaii)*

of Fort Barrette were emplaced in 1936 near Barbers Point. These structures still exist and resemble several other similar structures distributed in the heights around O'ahu, including those located on Ka'iwa Ridge in Lanikai.

An old soldier who served at station S in the late 1930s reports that for days on end he and a colleague lived at the station and were provisioned by Army pack mules. He told of unfortunate mules tripping and tumbling end-over-end down the mountain side. He said he and his colleague spent much of their time scanning the ocean with their telescope and reading magazines. The first thing he did every day was check in by telephone with the battery back at Fort Barrette.

World War II brought excitement to Ka'ena Point and the ridge overlooking the point. Every mile of O'ahu's coastline was to be fortified and Ka'ena Point was no exception. The first precaution taken after the December 7, 1941 attack was to emplace two surplus Navy 4-inch guns near the point.

These guns and others were frequently served by newly-trained soldiers, all draftees and recruits. One old veteran told about what happened to one such newly-minted soldier when they held a practice firing of these guns. Unnoticed by the gun commander, the soldier had positioned himself slightly downhill and in front of one of the guns. When it was fired, he was enveloped by the shock and rarefaction waves that accompanied the discharge. He was dead of his injuries when they found him. The firing of such guns was a deadly business for the careless.

As the war progressed, additional fortifications were started at the Point. Two searchlights were emplaced on the flanks of Pu'u Pueo and the construction of a two-gun battery of 8-inch guns was started but never completed before the war ended. Camp Kaena was constructed to house soldiers although now nothing remains of it.

The many concrete structures built on and into the flanks of Pu'u Pueo were abandoned when the war ended. A new era began for Ka'ena Point in 1958 when the military returned. It was the beginning of what became "Project Corona," a joint effort involving the Air Force, Navy, and Central Intelligence Agency.

Project Corona lasted until 1972 and involved earth satellites placed into orbit by Thor rockets launched at Vandenberg Air Force Base in California. The orbiting space capsules contained high-resolution cameras that could photograph the earth's surface over which the capsule passed. It was a Cold War project, and it takes no great imagination to conclude that many such photographs were taken of communist-occupied territory.

The exposed film was recovered in a very ingenious way. When it came time to recover the film, a signal was sent to the orbiting satellite from the transmitting station at Ka'ena Point. The film capsule separated from the satellite and retro-rockets slowed it down so that it began a descent into the earth's atmosphere where air drag slowed it further. Nine aircraft with special "recovery trapezes" were deployed to the predicted impact area about 600 miles west of O'ahu. Each aircraft was assigned to a sector within a ninety-by-thirty mile predicted-impact area, and Navy ships with helicopters carrying frog men were positioned to recover any capsule missed by the aircraft. Ka'ena Point radar tracked the descending capsule and assigned the nearest aircraft to the recovery.

Next the Ka'ena Point station sent a signal to the capsule at the appropriate time, ordering it to deploy a parachute. The nearest recovery aircraft then lowered its trapeze, made a pass at the slowly descending parachute-supported capsule, and pulled it into a cargo hold. The aircraft returned to Hickam Air Force Base where a waiting courier aircraft took the film to Washington for interpretation. This system was employed until satellite image-transmission made film recovery unnecessary after 1972.

Project Corona replaced the ancient departure of spirits with the arrival of data calculated to perpetuate the survival of the free world.

This completes the tour of West O'ahu.

END WORDS

HAWAI'I MOVED FROM a monarchy, to a republic, to a territory of the United States, and, finally became the fiftieth state admitted to the union, all in the short span of sixty-six years. The history of this movement is rich and colorful, and many records have been preserved to remind us of what it must have been like to live during those times. There is no better place to dig into this history than the Hawaii State Library, located at the corner of Punchbowl Street and King Street next to Iolani Palace.

Visit the Hawaii and Pacific Section of the library and browse the stacks. The section is roomy and air-conditioned and the librarians are there to assist you. Use the computer terminal to locate your favorite title. Tables and chairs are conveniently provided for leisurely research and copy machines are nearby. Holders of library cards can access the rare volumes kept in the reserve section under the care of librarians.

It is possible that reading this book has whetted your appetite for more about this unique state. A visit to the Hawaii and Pacific Section of the State Library will go far to satisfy your curiosity. Good hunting!

BIBLIOGRAPHY

The following were used as sources and all are recommended to the interested reader.

Barratt, Glynn, *The Russian Discovery of Hawaii—The Ethnographic and Historical Record,* Editions Limited, Honolulu, 1987.

Best, Gerald M., *Railroads of Hawaii...Narrow and Standard Gauge Common Carriers,* Golden West Books, San Mateo, California,1978.

Clark, John R. K., *The Beaches of Oahu,* A Kolowalu Book, The University Press of Hawaii, Honolulu, 1977.

Conde, Jesse C., and Gerald M. Best, *Sugar Trains; Narrow Gauge Rails of Hawaii,* Glenwood Publishing, Felton, California, 1973.

Day, A. Grove, *History Makers of Hawaii,* Mutual Publishing Company, Honolulu, 1984.

Department of Geography, University of Hawaii, *Second Edition Atlas of Hawaii,* University of Hawaii Press, Honolulu, 1983.

Devaney, Dennis M., Marion Kelly, Polly Jae Lee, and Lee S. Motteler, *Kaneohe—A History of Change,* The Bess Press, Honolulu, revised and updated October 1982.

Dorrance, William H., *Fort Kamehameha—The Story of the Harbor Defenses of Pearl Harbor,* White Mane Publishing Co., Inc., Shippensburg, Pa, 1993.

Forbes, David W., *Encounters With Paradise-Views of Hawaii and Its People,* Honolulu Academy of Arts, Honolulu, 1992.

Fornander, Abraham, *Ancient History of the Hawaiian People to the Times of Kamehameha I,* originally published as Volume II of *An Account of the Polynesian Race Its Origin and Migrations,* Mutual Publishing, Honolulu, 1996.

Gast, Ross H., *Don Francisco de Paula Marin,* The University Press of Hawaiʻi, Honolulu, 1973.

Gilmore, A. B., *The Hawaii Sugar Manual 1935-1936,* A. B. Gilmore, New Orleans, 1936.

Green, Peter, "Highway design tested by scenic Hawaii," ENR (magazine), December 7, 1992, pp. 25-30.

Hawaiian Historical Society, *The Hawaiian Journal of History,* an annual, The Hawaiian Historical Society, Honolulu, 1960-1997.

Hawaiian Sugar Planters' Association (now Hawaii Agriculture Research Center), *Hawaiian Sugar Manual 1991,* H.S.P.A., Aiea, Hawaiʻi, 1992.

Hibbard, Don, and David Franzen, *The View From Diamond Head-Royal Residence to Urban Resort,* Editions Limited, Honolulu, 1986.

Ii, John Papa, *Fragments of Hawaiian History,* Bishop Museum Press, Honolulu, 1959.

Joesting, Edward, *Tides of Commerce,* First Hawaiian, Inc., Honolulu, 1983.

Kamakau, S.M., *Ruling Chiefs of Hawaii-Revised Edition,* The Kamehameha Schools Press, Honolulu, 1992.

Kirch, Patrick Vinton, *Feathered Gods and Fishhooks An Introduction to Hawaiian Archaeology and Prehistory,* University of Hawaii Press, Honolulu, 1985.

Kuykendall, Ralph S., *The Hawaiian Kingdom, Volumes I, II, III,* University of Hawaii Press, Honolulu, 1938, 1953, and 1967.

Liliuokalani, Hawaii's Story by Hawaii's Queen, reprint, Charles E. Tuttle Company, Rutland, Vermont, 1964 (first edition, Lothrop, Lee and Shepard Company, Boston, 1898).

Nellist, George F., Ed., *The Story of Hawaii and Its Builders,* Honolulu Star-Bulletin, Ltd., Honolulu, 1925.

Melvin, Roy S. and Robert Ramsay, *Hawaiian Tramways,* booklet, *Pacific Railway Journal,* San Marino, California, 1961.

Prange, Gordon W., *At Dawn We Slept—The Untold Story of Pearl Harbor,* McGraw-Hill Book Company, New York, 1981.

Pukui, Mary Kawena, Samuel H. Elbert, and Esther T. Mookini, *Place Names of Hawaii,* University of Hawaii Press, Honolulu, 1974.

Schmitt, Robert C., and Ronn Ronck, *Firsts and Almost Firsts In Hawaii,* University of Hawaiʻi Press, Honolulu, 1995.

Snakenberg, Lokomaika'iokalani, "Oahu Pre-Mahele Moku and Ahupuaa," *Historic Hawai'i,* Volume 16, Number 6, June 1990.

Sterling, Elspeth, and Catherine C. Summers, *Sites of Oahu,* Bishop Museum Press, Honolulu, 1978.

Thrum, T. G., *Hawaiian Almanac and Annual,* Annually 1875-1891.

Thrum, T. G., *Hawaiian Annual,* annually 1892-1940.

U.S. Senate, *Coast Defenses of the United States and the Insular Possessions,* Senate Document 249, 59th Congress, 1st Session, March 6, 1906. "Taft Board Report."

Wordon, William L., *Cargoes-Matson's First Century in the Pacific,* The University Press of Hawaii, Honolulu, 1981.

Yardley, Paul T., *Millstones and Milestones, The Career of B. F. Dillingham,* University Press of Hawaii, Honolulu, 1981.

APPENDIX A

GLOSSARY

The reader will note the absence of "s" in the printed Hawaiian language. Hence all plural words lack an appended "s." *Heiau,* for example, can refer to a single, or a group, of Hawaiian temples.

Hawaiian Word	English Meaning
ahupua'a	land division of a district or *moku*
ali'i	royalty, high chiefs, or nobles
aloha	greeting, hello, good-bye, love
auwai	stream, streamlet, or ditch
ewa	toward the east, also a *moku*
haole	a Caucasian or white person, originally a stranger
hapai ko	lifting sugarcane
heiau	temple, place of worship or religious observance
hukilau	fishing with a seine or large net
hula	native dance

Hawaiian Word	English Meaning
kahuna	priest or wise man
kama'aina	a person born in Hawai'i
kapu	entry forbidden, iron rules
kiawe	algaroba tree
konohiki	head man, boss of *ahupua'a*
kuleana	small plot, land possession
lei	garland, usually of flowers around head or neck
loi	irrigated terrace
makahiki	autumn festival
makai	toward the ocean
mauka	inland, toward the mountains
mele	song
moku	land district, O'ahu was divided into six *moku*
pali	cliff or side of a mountain
pau	the end
poi	nourishing paste made from *taro*

HELPFUL INFORMATION

Hours change, phone for current hours.

Attraction	Phone	Days and Hours Open
Arizona Memorial	422-2771	Daily 7:30 to 5:00
Bishop Museum	847-3511	Daily 9:00 to 5:00
Fort Barrette	689-0168	City and County Ewa Complex Manager controls access
Hawai'i Maritime Museum	536-6373	Daily 8:30 to 5:00
Hawai'i's Plantation Village	676-6727	Daily 9:00 to 3:00 closed Sundays
Hawai'i Railway Society	681-5461	Mon.-Fri. 9:00 to noon Weekends 11:00 to 5:00
Hawai'i State Library Hawai'i. & Pacific Section	586-3535	Mon., Fri., Sat. 9:00-5:00 Tue. & Th. 9:00 to 8:00 Wed. 10:00 to 5:00
Polynesian Cultural Center	293-3333	Mon.-Sat. 12:30 to 9:00
Queen Emma Summer Palace	595-3167	Daily 9:00 to 4:00
Sea Life Park	259-7933	Mon.-Sat. 9:30 to 5:00
State Parks Information	587-0406	Mon.-Fri. 7:45-4:30

TheBus Information	848-5555	Daily, confirm bus routes here
Tropic Lightning Mus.	655-0438	Tues.-Sun. 10:00 to 4:30
U.S. Army Museum	438-2821	Tues.-Sun. 10:00 to 4:30
Waimea Valley Park	638-8511	Daily 10:00 to 5:30

APPENDIX B

Monarchs of the Kingdom of Hawai'i and missionaries and their descendents played key roles in O'ahu's history.

MONARCHS

Monarch	Born	Died	Ruled From	To
Kamehameha I	1758?	1819	1795	1819
Kamehameha II	1797	1824	1819	1824
Kamehameha III	1813	1854	1824	1854
Kamehameha IV	1834	1863	1855	1863
Kamehameha V	1830	1872	1863	1872
William C. Lunalilo	1832	1874	1873	1874
David Kalakaua	1836	1891	1874	1891
Lili'uokalani	1838	1917	1891	1893

The Republic of Hawai'i was formed on July 4, 1894 and Hawai'i was annexed to the United States July 7, 1898. Territorial government began June 14, 1900 with Sanford Ballard Dole as first governor. March 18, 1959 President Dwight D. Eisenhower signed the enabling act making Hawai'i the fiftieth state to be admitted to the United States.

MISSIONARIES

The American Board of Commissioners for Foreign Missions of Boston sent twelve companies of Congregationalist missionaries to Hawai'i between 1820 and 1848. The majority stayed and settled in Hawai'i and many of them and their descendents played key roles in Oahu's history down to the present.

First Company: Arrived March 21, 1820
Rev. and Mrs. Hiram Bingham, Rev. and Mrs. Asa Thurston, Dr. and Mrs. Thomas Holman, Mr. and Mrs. Samuel Whitney, Mr. and Mrs. Samuel Ruggles, Mr. and Mrs. Elisha Loomis, Mr. and Mrs. Daniel Chamberlain and five children. Native Hawaiians John Honolii, Thomas Hopu, William Kenui, and George Kaumuali'i, prince of Kauai, sailed with the company.

Second Company: Arrived April 27, 1823
Rev. and Mrs. Artemas Bishop, Mr. and Mrs. Abraham Bratchley, Mr. and Mrs. James Ely, Mr. and Mrs. Joseph Goodrich, Rev. and Mrs. William Richards, Rev. and Mrs. Charles S. Stewart, Miss Betsey Stockton, Mr. Stephen Popohe, Mr. William Kamooua, Mr. Richard Kalaialu, Mr. Kupelii.

Third Company: Arrived March 30, 1828
Rev. and Mrs. Lorrin Andrews, Rev. and Mrs. Ephraim W. Clark, Rev. and Mrs. Johnathan S. Green, Rev. and Mrs. Peter J. Gulick, Dr. and Mrs. Gerrit P. Judd, Miss Maria Ogden, Miss Maria Patten, Miss Delia Stone, Miss Mary Ward, Mr. and Mrs. Stephen Shepard, Mr. Henry Tahiti, Mr. Tyler Mills, and Mr. Phelps.

Fourth Company: Arrived June 7, 1831
Rev. and Mrs. Dwight Baldwin, Rev. and Mrs. Sheldon Dibble, Mr. and Mrs. Andrew Johnstone, and Rev. and Mrs. Rueben Tinker.

Fifth Company: Arrived May 17, 1832

Rev. and Mrs. William P. Alexander, Rev. and Mrs. Richard Armstrong, Dr. and Mrs. Alonzo Chapin, Rev. and Mrs. John S. Emerson, Rev. and Mrs. Cochran Forbes, Rev. and Mrs. David B. Lyman, Rev. and Mrs. Lorenzo Lyons, Mr. Edmund H. Rogers, Rev. and Mrs. Harvey Hitchcock, Rev. and Mrs. Ephraim Spaulding.

Sixth Company: Arrived May 1, 1833

Rev. and Mrs. John Diell, Rev. and Mrs. Benjamin W. Parker, Rev. and Mrs. Lowell Smith.

Seventh Company: Arrived June 6, 1835

Miss Lydia Brown, Rev. and Mrs. Titus Coan, Mr. and Mrs. Henry Dimond, Mr. and Mrs. Edwin O. Hall, and Miss Elizabeth M. Hitchcock.

Eighth Company: Arrived April 9, 1837

Dr. and Mrs. Seth L. Andrews, Mr. and Mrs. Edward Bailey, Rev. and Mrs. Isaac Bliss, Mr. and Mrs. Samuel N. Castle, Mr. and Mrs. Amos S. Cooke, Rev. and Mrs. Mark Ives, Mr. and Mrs. Edward Johnson, Mr. and Mrs. Horton O. Knapp, Dr. and Mrs. Thomas Lafon, Mr. and Mrs. Edwin Locke, Mr. and Mrs. Charles McDonald, Mr. and Mrs. Bethuel Munn, Miss Marcia M. Smith, Miss Lucia G. Smith, Mr. and Mrs. William S. Van Duzee, and Mr. and Mrs. Abner Wilcox.

Ninth Company: Arrived May 21, 1841

Rev. and Mrs. Elias Bond, Rev. and Mrs. Daniel Dole, Rev. and Mrs. John D. Paris, and Mr. and Mrs. William H. Rice.

Tenth Company: Arrived September 21, 1842

Rev. and Mrs. George B. Rowell and Dr. and Mrs. James W. Smith.

Eleventh Company: Arrived July 14, 1844

Rev. and Mrs. Claudius B. Andrews, Rev. and Mrs. Timothy D. Hunt, Rev. John F. Pogue, Miss Maria K. Whitney, and Rev. and Mrs. Eliphalet Whittlesey.

Twelfth Company: Arrived February 26, 1848
Rev. Samuel G. Dwight, and Rev. and Mrs. Henry Kinney.

Not every missionary came with the twelve companies. Others that came included:

The Rev. William Ellis in 1823, the Rev. Samuel C. Damon and wife in 1842, the Rev. Asa B. Smith and wife in 1843, Dr. Charles H. Wetmore and iwfe in 1849, the Rev. William C. Shipman and wife in 1854, the Rev. William O. Baldwin and wife and William A. Spooner and wife in 1855, the Rev. Anderson Forbes and wife in 1858, the Rev. Cyrus T. Mills and wife in 1860, the Rev. Sereno E. Bishop and wife in 1862, the Rev. William DeWitt Alexander and wife in 1865, the Rev. O. P. Emerson and wife in1889, and the Rev. John Leadingham and wife in 1894.

INDEX

ABOUT THE AUTHOR

William H. Dorrance is a historian and writer and author of the book, *Fort Kamehameha The Story of the Harbor Defenses of Pearl Harbor.* Several of his articles have appeared in *Historic Hawai'i* magazine and *The Hawaiian Journal of History* in addition to those featured in *Windward Oahu News.*

It was Lt. William H. Dorrance VI, then stationed at the Submarine Base at Pearl Harbor, who first encouraged his parents, the author and his wife, to visit Oʻahu hoping they would retire there. Lieutenant Dorrance's encouragement led to his parents' visit which resulted in their retirement on Oʻahu. Without their son's advice, production of this book would have been unlikely if not impossible.

Mr. and Mrs. Dorrance now reside in Kailua, Oʻahu.